I AM
WITH
YOU
ALWAYS

I AM WITH YOU ALWAYS

Reflections on the Church Year

Father Berard T. Doerger, O.F.M

Our Sunday Visitor Publishing Division
Our Sunday Visitor, Inc.
Huntington, Indiana 46750

Our Sunday Visitor Publishing Division
Our Sunday Visitor, Inc.
200 Noll Plaza
Huntington, Indiana 46750

International Standard Book Number: 0-87973-414-0
Library of Congress Catalog Card Number: 88-60923

Cover Design and Illustrations by Steve Windmiller

PRINTED IN THE UNITED STATES OF AMERICA

Table of Contents

Preface - Dedication

"BEHOLD, I AM with you always, until the end of the age" (Matthew 28, 20). From these closing words of Christ in the Gospel of St. Matthew I have chosen the title for this book on the liturgical year: *I AM WITH YOU ALWAYS*. For one of the important ways that Christ remains with us, his followers, "until the end of the age" is through and in the celebrations of the liturgical year of time. This liturgical year, like a spiral, leads always higher and with each turn takes us closer to the "end of the age" and to the last day, when Christ will come again in glory to make all things new.

The purpose of this book is to help us recognize and appreciate more clearly this presence of Christ among us in the seasons and feasts and celebrations of each liturgical season of the Church year.

In my own life, that recognition and appreciation of Christ's presence in the liturgical year was enkindled above all by the works of Father Pius Parsch, O.S.B., especially his commentary on the Church year, *Das Jahr des Heiles (The Church's Year of Grace)*. Much of the material of this present work will be based on the volumes of *Das Jahr des Heiles*.

And it is to the author of that work, Father Pius Parsch, that I gratefully dedicate this book.

> Father Berard Doerger, O.F.M.
> Hermitage of St. Anselm
> Houck, Arizona
> Feast of Christ the King, 1987

CHAPTER ONE

'CHRIST ... EVER LIVING IN HIS CHURCH'

(*Mediator Dei* of Pius XII)

Introduction to the Liturgical Year

SINCE I HAVE dedicated this book to Father Pius Parsch, the German Benedictine priest who popularized the liturgical renewal of the twentieth century, I would like to begin the study of the liturgical year with a quotation from the introduction to the twelfth edition (1937) of his most famous work, *Das Jahr des Heiles*. There he wrote the following about the Church or liturgical year:

> What a wonderful arrangement is the liturgical year! From whatever angle you consider it, it is beautiful and of great benefit for us humans. Oh that we would only use properly this great blessing of the liturgical year and fit it into the rhythm of our spiritual life![1]

The purpose of this opening chapter is to investigate as a

whole this "wonderful arrangement of the liturgical year," to trace in summary fashion its development over the centuries, and to highlight the "spirit" or "soul" of the liturgical year which is the true source of its beauty and which makes it such a "great blessing" and benefit to us Christians.

Thus, this chapter will have three sections: the "body" or external elements that make the liturgical year as we observe it today in the post-Vatican II Church; a brief history of the development of the liturgical year; and finally, the "soul" or "spirit" of the liturgical year.

I. The 'Body' of the Liturgical Year

Most of the material in this section on the "body" or external elements of the liturgical year is based on the Second Vatican Council document *The Constitution on the Sacred Liturgy (Sacrosanctum Concilium*, nn. 102-111). This was the first document produced by the Council and was promulgated by Pope Paul VI on December 4, 1963.

As a general definition of the liturgical year in its exterior or visible garb, we can say that the liturgical year is the celebration of the principal events of our redemption by devoutly recalling these events on certain days and seasons throughout each year (cf. *SC*, n. 102). Or, as Adolf Adam describes the liturgical year in his book by that name, "The liturgical year is the commemorative celebration, throughout a calendar year, of the saving deeds God accomplished in Jesus Christ."[2]

This Church or liturgical year is not to be seen, we should state from the beginning, as something entirely different from, or as a rival to, the civil or calendar year. Time is itself a gift of God the Creator, and, as we will see later, the liturgical year is simply the sanctifying or gracing of "secular time" by God's becoming present to us in time. To quote Adolf Adam again, "All time has become God's time and a time of salvation, since God's offer of salvation is directed to all periods of history and all human beings."[3]

The Commemorative Celebration of the Pascal Mystery and Other Mysteries of Christ

To return to our definition: the liturgical year is the celebration of the principal events of our redemption by devoutly recalling these events on certain days and seasons of the year. The chief mystery or event of our redemption that we recall and celebrate is the paschal or Easter mystery of Christ; i.e., his passing through death on the cross to new life in the Resurrection. Every week, on the day we call "The Lord's Day," we recall and celebrate the resurrection of Christ the Lord. The Church also celebrates the Lord's resurrection, together with his blessed passion and death, at Easter, the most solemn festival of the Church year.

During the rest of the year, the Church celebrates the other mysteries or events of Christ's life, beginning with the mystery of the Incarnation and Birth of Christ and progressing through the events of his public life and work, until the Ascension, Christ's sending of the Holy Spirit on the Church, and ending with the expectation of the blessed hope of the Second Coming of the Lord at the end of time (cf. *SC*, n. 102).

Special Recalling and Honoring Mary and the Memory of the Saints

In celebrating this yearly cycle of Christ's mysteries, the Church in the course of the liturgical year also recalls and honors with special love the Blessed Mary, the Mother of Christ, "who is joined," says the liturgy document, "by an inseparable bond to the saving work of her Son" (n. 103). In Mary, then, the Church is admiring and holding up for imitation the most excellent fruit of the saving work of Christ. It is important for us to note that honor is given to Mary because of her close connection with Christ and with the whole mystery of redemption.

Also included in the liturgical year are days devoted to the memory of the martyrs and other saints. "By celebrating the passage of these saints from earth to heaven," says the *Constitution on the Liturgy*, "the Church proclaims the paschal mystery achieved in the saints who have suffered and been glorified with Christ; and she proposes them to the faithful as examples drawing all to the Father through Christ, and through their merits she pleads for God's favor" (n. 105). In these words I think we find the theological foundations for proper devotion to the saints and their place in the liturgical year and in our lives: (a) through their merits the Church pleads for God's favor; (b) they are examples for us, drawing all to the Father through Christ; and most importantly, (c) the celebration of the life and death of the saints is a proclamation of the paschal mystery of Christ achieved in them.

The Four Cycles of the Liturgical Year

This, then, is the basic outline of the "body" or exterior form of the liturgical year. It is the commemorative celebration, throughout a calendar year of the saving deeds God accomplished in Jesus Christ. We structure this commemorative celebration today in these cycles:

+ The Christmas Cycle, in which we commemorate and celebrate Christ's coming into the world as one like us;
+ The Easter Cycle, in which we commemorate the redemption that Christ brought to the world through his passion and resurrection;
+ The Temporal Cycle (Season of Ordinary Time), during which "the mystery of Christ in all its fullness is celebrated." (In this cycle we also find certain "feasts of ideas." These feasts do not focus directly on particular events of salvation, but rather focus on particular truths of our faith or special aspects of Christian teaching or piety. Some of these "feasts of ideas" are the Feast of the Holy Trinity, Corpus Christi, the Feast of the Sacred Heart, etc.);
+ The Sanctoral Cycle or calendar of the feasts of Mary and the oth-

er saints, in which we pointed out earlier, we celebrate the paschal mystery of Christ achieved in them.

Sometimes this exterior form or structure of the liturgical year is compared to the structure of a cathedral. In drawing out this comparison, the Easter Cycle forms the central nave or most important part of the cathedral; the Christmas Cycle is the atrium or vestibule of the cathedral; and the Sanctoral Cycle functions as a circlet of small chapels around the nave.

Father Pius Parsch, who wrote before the reform of the liturgical year by Vatican II, uses a little different comparison. He compares the external form of the liturgical year to some of the old monasteries in Austria. In these monasteries there is the original building, and then there are many sections added on to the monastery over the centuries, and various connecting links made between buildings. Also various styles of architecture are apparent in the different sections, sometimes disguising the original building and its architecture. There are also various courtyards and gardens surrounding the monastery buildings. These latter Father Parsch compares to the feasts of Mary and the saints. The original building, says Parsch, is the original liturgy of the Church (the celebration of the paschal mystery), and then the other additions to the monastery are the feasts of Christ and the seasons that developed over the centuries and became part of the liturgical year.

That development of the liturgical year over the centuries is what we want to consider in more detail in our next section.

II. Brief History of the Development of the Liturgical Year

The liturgical year is not something that was given to the twelve apostles by Christ, nor is it something that was carefully planned out step by step from the first years of the Church. Rather, the liturgical year is something that has grown and developed over the centuries, guided, I think we can say, by the Holy Spirit.

The Memorial of the Lord

The first Christians began to celebrate simply "The Memorial of the Lord." They gathered together for prayer and "the breaking of the bread"; and this "breaking of the bread," a name for the Mass, was then as it is now the "memorial," the calling to mind and making present the death and glorification of Christ. Sunday, the day of Christ's resurrection, was soon chosen as *the* day each week to celebrate this memorial of the Lord. And soon the Easter Feast was established as *the* feast of salvation, *the* celebration of the passing of Christ from death to resurrection.

Thus, the paschal mystery of Christ, his passing over or through death to life is the "heart" of the liturgical year. The heart, as you know, is the principal organ of the body that supplies all areas of the body, even the smallest parts, with the blood that is needed for life. The heart signifies the innermost core or center of an organism and is the starting point and terminus or end-point of the circulating blood. So, too, the paschal mystery is the heart of the liturgical year, and all the other parts of the liturgical year derive nourishment and growth and meaning from this central mystery of the death and resurrection of Christ.[4]

The Easter Season

Around this central feast of Christ's resurrection there developed gradually a longer season of Easter. Already in the apostolic times the Feast of Pentecost came to be celebrated as the conclusion of the Easter celebration. Next the custom arose of having some days and weeks of preparation for the Easter Feast through fasting and prayer and also special instructions for those to be baptized at the Easter Vigil service. We now call this period of preparation the season of "Lent." In the fourth century Christians began to commemorate the "holy triduum" of Holy Thursday, Good Friday, and Holy Saturday. By the sixth century, the beginning of Lent and of the whole Easter Season had been placed back as far as Septuagesima Sunday (about seventy days before the actual Easter Sunday). This Septuagesima Sunday was also then considered as the beginning of the liturgical year as it was known at that time.

The Christmas-Epiphany Season

The other lesser season or cycle of the liturgical year, the Christmas-Epiphany cycle, had its roots back in the fourth century and gradually grew into the Christmas season that we know today. Originally it seems that this Christmas-Epiphany season was considered as the conclusion of the Church year, with its emphasis focused on the last things and the expectation of the Second Coming of Christ as King at the end of time. Epiphany, especially in the Eastern Church, was the original center-point or main feast of this season and not the birth of Christ. But, as we said, the "parousia" or Second Coming of Christ was the mystery that received the greatest emphasis.

In the course of time, however, the Birth of Christ and his Incarnation came to the foreground of this feast and cycle, and gradually the whole childhood of Jesus was associated with this cycle or season. And, from this development followed fairly naturally the decisions to consider Advent (the period of preparation for the Christmas Feast) the beginning of the liturgical year since this cycle of Advent-Christmas-Epiphany celebrated the beginnings of Christ's life and his work of salvation. (Advent, as a time of preparation for Christmas, began in Spain and Gaul around the fifth century.)

The Development of the "Connecting Corridors" and Other Feasts

Another phase of development of the liturgical year was the phase that connected together the two buildings or cycles of the liturgical year. Two corridors, as it were, were built: the one, the six Sundays after Epiphany; and the other longer one, the twenty-four Sundays after Pentecost. This was done at the beginning of the Middle Ages.

In our present-day reform of the liturgical year these connecting links or corridors have been torn down to some extent and have been replaced by what is called "The Season of Ordinary Time." This season begins at the end of the Christmas Cycle (The Baptism of Our Lord) and extends to Ash Wednesday, the start of the Easter Cycle. It then takes up again at the end of the Easter Cycle (the feast of Pentecost) and continues until the First Sunday of Advent. Thus, this Season of Ordinary Time now forms a unit of thirty-three to thirty-four weeks.

One other development in the liturgical year over the centuries was the establishment of other feasts of our Lord and feasts of the Blessed Mother and the other saints of the Church. This development has continued into our own day.

The Renovation of the Liturgical Year by the Second Vatican Council

To complete our treatment of the history of the growth and development of the liturgical year, we should add that one of the greatest renovations of the liturgical year has taken place in our own era as a consequence of the Second Vatican Council and the *Constitution on the Liturgy*, the first document published by the Council. The Fathers of the Council in that document on the liturgy decreed that the liturgical year was to be revised "so that the traditional customs and desciplines of the sacred season shall be preserved or restored to suit the conditions of modern times" — renovation and adaptation! The Fathers of the Council emphasized the importance of the Lord's Day as being the original feast day of the Church and directed that the feasts of the Lord and the Proper of the Time be given due preference over the feasts of the saints. They also decreed that the two elements especially characteristic of Lent, recalling of baptism or preparation for it and penance, be given greater emphasis in this season. Finally,they urged that the list of saints' feasts be reduced and only those should be extended to the universal Church who are truly of universal importance (cf. nn. 106-111).

So what has happened in our century is, I would say, a complete renovation and modernization of the liturgical year, almost from top to bottom, so that the liturgical year now has a more definite unity and proportion to it. Certain of the original features have been restored, but all have been adapted to fit our present day and age.

III. The 'Spirit' or 'Soul' of the Liturgical Year

Thus far, we have been treating of the body or the exterior, visible elements that make up the liturgical year, just as we might study the ordinary calendar year and see how it is put together with twelve months, four seasons, 365 days, etc. There is more to the liturgical year, however, than just this "body" or physical arrangement of seasons and feasts. There is also a "soul" or "spirit" of the liturgical year which we cannot as such see. Hence, when we treat of this aspect of the liturgical year, we are very much in the area of faith.

Aim or Purpose of the Liturgical Year

To understand the spirit or soul of the liturgical year, let us look first at the aim or purpose of the liturgical year.

This aim or purpose is not simply a historical review of the life of Christ or the history of salvation. It is not just a recalling of the past events of salvation, nor merely a placing before us the historical lives of holy men and women who lived throughout the centuries of the Church's existence. The liturgical year generally announces or proclaims not the past but the present, and it also looks to the future. It offers us not history (*Geschichte*) but happening (*Geschehen*), i.e., things taking place right now. The liturgical year doesn't want to relate past deeds simply as past deeds; rather, it wants to give and develop supernatural life in us right now in the present. The purpose or aim of the liturgical year is, then, the same essential goal as that of the Church itself and of Christ's coming to earth: namely, that we "might have life and have it more abundantly" (John 10:10).

Certainly the liturgical year does take us back into the past: the Old Testament with its main figures and events are set before us; the chief historical events in Christ's life are related; and the heroic lives of the saints are recalled for us. All these things are past deeds. Yet, this past, this history, is only, as it were, the outer garment or covering; it is only a picture and symbol for the present. The relating of these past events is the "body" of the Church year; the "soul" is the development of divine life, of Christ's life, within us. The Old Testament is recalled in order to show us the fulfillment of its message in the New Testament and in our own times; the historical life of Christ renews itself in our own lives through the bestowal of Christ's grace and life now in the present; and the saints, most of whom are long dead, are expected to share with us from the fullness of their glorified lives.

Christ Himself Ever Living in His Church

Pope Pius XII in his Encyclical on the Sacred Liturgy brought out this above idea quite clearly when he wrote that the liturgical year "is not a cold and lifeless representation of the events of the past, or a simple and bare historical record of a former age. It is rather Christ himself who is ever living in his Church. . . . Here [in the liturgical year] he continues that journey of immense mercy which he began in his earthly life, going about doing good. This he does in order to bring the souls of all into contact with his mysteries, and so make them live by them. These mysteries are now constantly present and active . . . each of them is, according to its own way, the cause of our salvation."[5]

Adolf Adam in his book *The Liturgical Year*, which we referred to earlier, tries to clarify this truth of Christ's presence in the liturgical year by comparing it to the sun. "The sun," he says, "ceaselessly emits its wealth of light and heat throughout the centuries and on every continent, city, and village. It has done this for millions of years without ever exhausting its energy or diminishing its brilliance. In similar fashion Christ and his redemptive action have become a new sun of salvation; he emits his rays wherever a community gathers for its liturgical celebration and opens itself to him in faith and love. Thus he fulfills his promise: 'Where two or three are gathered in my name, there am I in the midst of them' (Matthew 18:20)."[6]

Thus, the liturgical year is not just an edifying commemoration of the past, but a making real in the present for the sake of a future.[7] In other words, the saving acts of Christ that we commemorate here and now become present to us because their consequences and effects are prolonged in time and become actualized for us now. For example, the celebration of Christmas is not a simple remembering of the birth of Christ in the stable at Bethlehem, but the celebration actualizes, makes present the birth of Christ "for us." Pope St. Leo the Great put it this way: "Although the series of bodily actions is now past, as ordained in the eternal plan . . . nevertheless we adore the virgin birth that brings us salvation."[8] Our remembering of what Jesus did (his birth, death, resurrection, etc.) is a remembrance that enables us to share in the mysteries of Christ. That sun, that we talked about in the previous paragraph, continues to shine for us here and now through our celebration of these historical events of Christ's life. Those mysteries are constantly present and active, as Pope Pius XII said, and they make Christ's saving deeds, his salvation, available to us.

As we consider each season of the liturgical year in the chapters ahead, we will try to specify in more detail the manner that Christ remains ever living and active in his Church in these seasons of the liturgical year.

The Sacramental Character of the Liturgical Year

The ideas expressed above about the spirit or soul of the liturgical year can be expressed in another way by speaking of the "sacramental character" of the liturgical year. (We are using the word "sacrament" here in its wider meaning, wider than just the seven sacraments, as is frequently done in theology today, and as it was used in the Church in the early centuries.)

A "sacrament" can be defined as "a divine bestowal of salvation in an outwardly perceptible form; a bestowal of salvation (grace) in historical visibility" (Schillebeeckx). This definition contains two important elements: (a) a becoming-present, a meeting, a "nearing" of God — God coming to us in some perceptible form — and (b) a gracing, a sanctifying of a human being — a person becomes holy, filled with divine life.

In this sense of the word "sacrament," the first and greatest sacrament is *Christ* himself. In Christ we have a becoming-present of God, a meeting of God with the human race in the perceptible form of Christ's human nature. And, there is a "gracing," a sanctification of human nature through this incarnation of Christ.

The second great sacrament is the *Church*. (The *Constitution on the Liturgy* speaks of the Church as a "wondrous sacrament" in Article 5.) In the Church, which is the mystical body of Christ, God also draws near to the human race. Wherever the Church steps into the world through its missionaries and preachers, its priests and its lay people, there do God and Christ become present. And the Church also fills human beings with the graces of salvation through its activities.

This sacramental activity of the Church extends to all that lies within the Church's sacred realm; hence, to space, to time, to persons, and to things. The liturgical year, then, is nothing more than *time sanctified and graced by Christ and his Church*. In this way the liturgical year takes part in the sacramental character of the Church itself.

The liturgical year has this character of a sacrament since

it contains the two elements we spoke of above: (a) God appears, he becomes present in time; he steps from eternity, as it were, into our human time (the hour, a day, a season, the whole year); and (b) God doesn't come into time empty-handed, but he sanctifies time; he purifies it and fills it with his grace and life. It thus becomes a hallowed time, a sacred time or season or year. Hence, another way of describing the spirit or soul of the liturgical year is to say it is "the grace-filled entering of God into our time" ("*gnadenvolles Eintreten Gottes in unsere Zeit*" — Parsch). The eternal God enters into our time, our lives here and now, and fills this time with his divine life!

Conclusion

To sum up some of the main points of this chapter, we can say that the various feasts and seasons of the liturgical year are not a mere festive remembrance of the saving acts of Christ and his saints, but these feasts and seasons bring us the real presence of Christ and the here-and-now application of the saving deeds of Christ. The individual and the entire community enter into a fuller communion with Christ and the life that he came to bring us and which he wishes us to possess in its fullness.

And, we should add, each liturgical year carries us closer to Christ and the final coming of Christ in glory at the end of time. Hence, it is not appropriate to compare the liturgical year with a circle or a ring which always returns to its starting point and then sets out again. A better comparison for the liturgical year is that of a spiral staircase or the thread of a wood screw, in which each turn leads one higher. Thus, each liturgical year leads always higher, and each turn carries one a bit further from the starting point and on towards Christ's fullness. One liturgist (T. Kampmann) has put it this way: "First, no liturgical year is exactly like any other; and, secondly, each cycle moves closer to the parousia, the last day, and the life of the world to come."[9]

* * * * * * *

CHAPTER TWO

'THY KINGDOM COME!'

(Matthew 6, 10)

The Season of Advent

THE LITURGICAL year begins with the First Sunday of Advent, which is the period of preparation for the feast of Christmas. In the review of the historical development of the liturgical year in the previous chapter, we mentioned that the season of Advent was first celebrated in the latter part of the fifth century in Spain and Gaul. In Rome, the beginnings of an Advent liturgy are first evident in the middle of the sixth century.

The Spirit or Character of Advent

As we study the history of the liturgical year we find that the focus of Advent as well as the spirit of the season has varied in different ages and among various cultures. At times the eschatological theme of Christ's second coming was emphasized over the incarnational theme of Christ's birth; and in some cultures Advent was viewed as more of a penitential season in contrast to a period of joyful preparation and expectation for the birth of Christ into the world.

The latest *General Norms for the Liturgical Year* (n. 39) say this about the meaning and character of the season of Advent in the present arrangement of the liturgical year: "This season has a twofold character. It is a time of preparation for Christmas when the first coming of God's Son to the world is recalled. It is also a season when minds are directed by this memorial to Christ's second coming at the end of time. It is thus a season of joyful and spiritual expectation."

This statement gives us the basic character and spirit of the Advent season for the Church today. It is first of all a period of preparation for the festive remembrance or memorial of Christ's first coming into the world and his birth in Bethlehem. But the joyful recalling of this first coming of Christ serves as a springboard to direct our attention to Christ's promised second coming at the end of time. The Advent season, then, is a season of hope, of expectation, of longing, colored throughout with a spirit of joy!

Advent is, of course, just part of the longer season or cycle of Christmas, which cycle ends now on the Feast of the Baptism of the Lord. The four weeks of Advent are the period of preparation and expectation; then there follows the period of solemn celebration from Christmas Day to the Epiphany. And there are other celebrations that help to expand the memorial of the birth and early life of Jesus: the Feast of the Holy Family (first Sunday after Christmas); the Solemnity of Mary (January 1); and the Feast of the Holy Innocents (December 28). The Baptism of the Lord (the Sunday after the Epiphany) serves as a fitting conclusion of this Christmas Cycle, since this event brought the hidden life of Jesus to an end and, at the same time, marked the beginning of his public life and teaching. The cycle of the liturgical year known as the Ordinary Time of the Year, which begins immediately after the Feast of the Baptism of the Lord, then

24

pursues and recalls this public phase of Christ's life upon earth.

The Three Comings of Christ

The word "Advent" is derived from the Latin word "*Adventus*," which is translated into English as "coming." The word is said to be a term borrowed from the pagans and was first used by the Christians for the feast or event of Christmas itself. Later it was extended to the preparation period for the feast of Christmas, acquiring the overtones of "expectation for the coming of Christ."[1]

There are three "comings" that the liturgy of Advent intends to prepare us for during this season. The first coming that we prepare to celebrate is Christ's coming in the flesh, his *historical or incarnational coming* as a human being into the world in David's town of Bethlehem in the land of Judah.

This mystery of Christ's incarnational coming, however, is made present and active again, as Pope Pius XII stated in his encyclical *Mediator Dei*, by his continued coming to us in our own time: his *sacramental coming* through the life of grace, given to us in our liturgical celebration of the historical coming. Christ becomes flesh as it were in us; he is born anew in us, the members of his body, the Church. This is the coming of which Christ himself spoke when he said: "Whoever loves me will keep my word, and my Father will love him, and we will come to him and make our dwelling place with him" (John 14, 23).

At the same time, Christ's sacramental coming in grace to us now and the memorial of his first or historical coming anticipate and awaken within us the hope and yearning for Christ's *final coming in glory*; and the first two comings prepare us for that "day of the Lord" at the end of time.

Thus, in the Advent liturgy, the past, present, and future are all marvelously blended together as we prepare and await in hope and joy for the coming of "Jesus Christ . . . the same yesterday, today, and forever" (Hebrews 13, 8). St. Bernard speaks beautifully of these three comings of Christ in a sermon used for the Office of Readings on Wednesday of the first week of Advent:

> We know that there are three comings of the Lord. The third lies between the other two. It is invisible, while the other two are visible. In the first coming he was seen on earth, dwelling among men; he himself testifies that they saw him and hated him. In the final coming "all flesh will see the salvation of our God" and "they will look on him whom they pierced." The intermediate coming is a hidden one; in it only the elect see the Lord within their own selves, and they are saved. In his first coming our Lord came in our flesh and in our weakness; in this middle coming he comes in spirit and power; in the final coming he will be seen in glory and majesty.

The Symbol of Light in the Advent Liturgy

The chief symbol that is used to describe these three comings of Christ in the liturgy of Advent and of the whole Christmas Cycle is the symbol of "light" and the "sun." Christ is the light shining in the darkness, a light which gives light and life to every person (cf. John 1, 5-9). The whole Christmas Cycle is a season of light and of the sun. At dawn of the First Sunday of Advent, the reading at Morning Prayer proclaims: "It is now the hour for you to rise from sleep . . . the night is far advanced; the day draws near. Let us cast off the deeds of darkness and put on the armor of light" (Romans 13, 11-12).

This dawning light (Christ) rises and grows in brilliance throughout the weeks of Advent, and from Christmas through Epiphany it shines in all its radiance as the "Sol invictus," the Unconquerable Sun that is the true and only light of the world, scattering the darkness of sin and bringing the light of life and love to all. The liturgical texts for the Masses and the Liturgy of the Hours for these days from Christmas to Epiphany are filled with this theme and symbol of light. Perhaps the passage from Chapter 60 of Isaiah is the most effusive:

Rise up in splendor [O Jerusalem]! Your light has come,
the glory of the Lord shines upon you.
See, darkness covers the earth,
and thick clouds cover the peoples;
But upon you the LORD shines,
and over you appears his glory.
Nations shall walk by your light,
and kings by your shining radiance.

(Isaiah 60, 1-3)

Even in the final feast of this Christmas Cycle, the Baptism of the Lord, the theme of light is present in several places in the liturgy for this feast. The first reading at Mass contains the line from Isaiah: "I formed you and set you as a covenant of the people, a light for the nations, to open the eyes of the blind, to bring prisoners from confinement, and from the dungeon, those who live in darkness" (Isaiah 42, 6-7). And St. Gregory Nazianzus, in the Office of Readings, speaks of the baptism of Christ as a bathing in light, and he urges us to be bathed in this light. He ends his sermon with these words:

> He wants you to become a living force for all mankind, lights shining in the world. You are to be radiant lights as you stand beside Christ, the great light, bathed in the glory of him who is the light of heaven. You are to enjoy more and more the pure and dazzling light of the Trinity, as now you have received — though not in its fullness — a ray of its splendor, proceeding from the one God, in Christ Jesus our Lord, to whom be glory and power for ever and ever. Amen.

The Church's Heralds of the Advent Season

A herald is a forerunner, a messenger who proclaims and announces the coming of a king to visit some city of his kingdom or to proclaim other important news. During the period of Advent, the Church's liturgy (i.e., the Sunday and weekday Mass texts and the texts of the Liturgy of the Hours) presents us with three principal heralds. These heralds alert and excite and prepare us for the memorial of Christ's first coming almost two thousand years ago, the experiencing of his sacramental coming in the present, and the expectation of his final coming in glory at the end of time.[2]

1. The Herald of Hope and Expectation: The Prophet Isaiah

The first of these heralds is the Prophet Isaiah, and he is the herald of hope and expectation.

During the four weeks of Advent, the first readings at the Sunday and weekday Masses and the majority of the Scripture readings in various hours of the Liturgy of the Hours are from the Old Testament books of the Bible. And prominent by far in these readings are selections from the Book of the Prophet Isaiah — almost a hundred selections throughout this Advent season. The prophet Isaiah, therefore, stands as *the* representative and herald for the Old Testament during this season.

And what is the chief function or purpose of the pronouncements from Isaiah during this period of Advent? Their principal purpose seems to be to awaken and stir into flame within us a lively hope, an eager desire, an intense expectation and longing for the coming of the Messiah. The cry of Isaiah, "Let the clouds rain down the just one and earth bud forth a Savior (*'Rorate caeli desuper*, etc.')," expresses that hope and longing; and these words have become one of the favorite Advent prayers and songs of Christianity.

But what is it that we Christians are to hope and yearn for and await with eagerness? *It is Christ and the fullness of his kingdom in the Church, in the world and in our individual lives.* This is not to say that we hope for and pray for Christ's coming as if God has not yet sent his Son among us, as if we had not yet received him. No, that would be play-acting and a dangerous psychological and theological viewpoint, as Father Nocent warns in his book on the Liturgical Year.[3] That same author points out that as Christians we hope in a certain sense for what we already possess. We already hold Christ in our hand; in baptism we have died and risen with Christ and already received a share in his life; we already possess the rudiments or first fruits of our own glory and of the world to come.

Yet, as Christians still in this world, we know that we still await the face-to-face encounter with the Christ who is promised to us and whom we already possess; we still long and hope and wait for the mirror to be broken and to see Christ face to face, sharing in the fullness of His glory. And so each year, writes Father Nocent, "the Church puts the Christian into a situation where his hope can come alive and grow strong; she bids him hope, along with the whole of the Old Testament for the coming of deliverance. The deliverance has already been accomplished; now he can celebrate it as a deliverance that is present to him through signs, and as he celebrates it, he can reach out for, and make his way toward, that moment when all signs shall vanish. The element of waiting that is part of Christian hope finds sacramental expression as the Christian relives in the present the Old Testament past, lives the incarnation as an event of today, and waits for the return of Christ and breaking of the mirror on the last day."[4]

It is the Prophet Isaiah who is for us the Church's principal herald of hope and longing and expectation in Advent, which is sometimes called "the season of hope."

The Herald of Repentance and Purification: John the Baptist

Another prophet who plays an important role in the liturgy's preparation of Christians for the coming of Christ is the last and greatest of the prophets, John the Baptist. God had made John the herald and forerunner of the first coming of Christ. And the Church in its Advent liturgy now makes John the herald and forerunner of Christ's coming in grace and his coming at the end of time. Isaiah prepares us for Christ's coming as a herald of hope, stirring up a longing and eager expectation for Christ;

John prepares us for Christ's coming as a herald of repentance, urging upon us a desire for reform and purification of our lives, so that we are prepared and worthy to meet our King and welcome him into our hearts.

John's chief message to us is the same as it was to the Jewish people of his time, "Repent, for the kingdom of heaven is at hand!" (Matthew 3, 2), and quoting Isaiah: "Prepare the way of the Lord, make straight his paths. Every valley shall be filled and every mountain and hill shall be made low. The winding roads shall be made straight, and the rough ways made smooth, and all flesh shall see the salvation of God" (Luke 3, 3-6). Repentance of sin, reform and transformation of our spiritual lives, purification of our heart and attitudes, growth in holiness — these are the tasks that John the Baptist calls us to as we prepare for Christ's coming.

Some of the second readings at the Sunday Masses of Advent echo and spell out in greater detail John's call to repentance and purification. We give here a sampling:

"Let us then throw off the works of darkness [and] put on the armor of light; let us conduct ourselves properly as in the day, not in orgies and drunkenness, not in promiscuity and licentiousness, not in rivalry and jealousy. But put on the Lord Jesus Christ. . ." (Romans 13, 12-14).

"May the God of endurance and encouragement grant you to think in harmony with one another, in keeping with Christ Jesus. . ." (Romans 15, 5).

"Since everything is to be dissolved in this way, what sort of persons ought [you] to be, conducting yourselves in holiness and devotion, waiting for and hastening the coming of the day of God. . ." (2 Peter 3, 11).

"And this is my prayer: that your love may increase ever more and more in knowledge and every kind of perception, to discern what is of value, so that you may be pure and blameless for the day of Christ. . ." (Philippians 1, 9-10).

"Rejoice in the Lord always. I shall say it again: rejoice! Your kindness should be known to all. The Lord is near" (Philippians 4, 4-5).

"May the Lord make you increase and abound in love for one another and for all, just as we have for you, so as to strengthen your hearts, to be blameless in holiness before our God and Father at the coming of our Lord Jesus with all his holy ones" (1 Thessalonians 3, 12-13).

Thus, during Advent, John the Baptist leads the way in urging us to prepare for the Lord by *turning away* from the darkness of sin and selfishness of all kinds and *turning toward* God in prayer and in putting on the Lord Jesus Christ by our holy and blameless lives, living in love and harmony with all. One of the psalm antiphons used repeatedly in the Liturgy of the Hours during Advent summarizes well the exhortations of John and the liturgy of Advent in general: "Let us cleanse our hearts for the coming of our great King, that we may be ready to welcome him; he is coming and will not delay."

3. The Herald of Joy and Union with God: The Blessed Mary
The prophet Isaiah is the Church's herald of hope and expectation for the coming of the Messiah; John the Baptist is the herald of repentance and purification for us as we prepare for the coming of Christ; and the third herald of Christ's coming that the Church presents to us in these weeks of Advent is the "virgin betrothed to a man named Joseph, of the house of David, and the virgin's name was Mary" (Luke 1, 27).

Mary had been the special temple prepared by Christ for the coming of his Son into the human world. It was in her body that God took on flesh, that he became like us, that he became "God-with-us, Emmanuel!" The liturgy now uses Mary during this Advent season as the herald of joy and union with God. "My spirit rejoices in God my Savior. For he has looked with favor upon his handmaid's lowliness" (Luke 1, 46). Mary becomes the personification of the purpose and goal of Advent: to be united with Christ and God and to share in the fullness of Christ's joy and in his very nature as God.

Throughout the four weeks of Advent, Mary is kept before our eyes in the liturgy, especially in the antiphons at the various hours of the Divine Office. A sampling:

"The Holy Spirit will come upon you, Mary; you have no need to be afraid. You will carry in your womb the Son of God, alleluia."

"This is the good news the prophets foretold: The Savior will be born of the Virgin Mary."

"The angel said to Mary in greeting: Hail, full of grace, the Lord is with you; blessed are you among women."

"Blessed are you, O Virgin Mary, for your great faith; all that the Lord promised you will come to pass through you, alleluia."

In the final days of Advent, Mary is constantly featured in the liturgy, especially in the Gospel selections during those final days of preparation. (The Feast of the Immaculate Conception on December 8, though not officially part of the Advent liturgy, fits beautifully into this season as we recall God's preserving Mary from all sin so that she might be a fitting temple for his Son.)

Father Parsch writes of Mary and her role in Advent in these words:

It is a special sign of God's goodness and love that he has put the work of our salvation into such a human framework. The Redeemer was to be a human being like us, subject to the needs and wants of the natural order. He was to be conceived and born like us. All this shows how God was willing to meet us in the work of salvation, not as God to be feared, but rather as a true Emmanuel (God-with-us). Then, too, he chose a woman to collaborate with him. His plan was so wonderful and heart-warming that it is easily understandable why the Church never lets this mystery out of sight. Constantly she places before us the beautiful picture of the Mother with her divine child. Now can we understand why the Church wants us to go through Advent with Mary and in the spirit of Mary? Since Advent is in the first place a preparation for the coming of Christ in grace to us, who can be a better model than Mary, who bore Christ in her own body and sheltered him and was privileged to be a mother for him? Yes, the mystery of Mary's divine motherhood, the most perfect example of God's indwelling, demands an extensive role in the liturgy of this season.[5]

Isaiah, John the Baptist, and the Virgin Mary: What a wonderful group of heralds and models for our observance of Advent! And what a glorious message and exhortation they deliver to us: Hope and yearn for him! Prepare and purify your hearts for him! Rejoice in him who comes to live within you!

"Thy Kingdom Come"

We mentioned earlier in this chapter that we must not hope and prepare for Christ's coming in Advent as if he had never come or as if we had not yet received him. Christ has come into the world and into our lives. We hope and prepare for what we already possess, but we hope and prepare for Christ's fuller coming into this world of ours and into our individual lives.

Father Parsch, in his introduction to the Advent season, suggests that to avoid any artificiality and insincerity in our longing and preparing for the coming of the Lord, we might substitute the theme of the "coming of the kingdom" in place of the "coming of the Lord." I have personally found this suggestion a

most fruitful way of living in the Advent spirit of hope and repentance and joy, and so I translate and present Father
Parsch's suggestion here:

A practical idea occurs to me which should lend to Advent an
impetus of great value in our present-day celebration of this season. As the object of our longing, let us substitute the "coming of
the kingdom" in place of the "coming of the Lord." The Lord has
indeed come many years ago and we cannot long for him personally to come again as a human being, but his kingdom is always
coming and will come in its fullness only at the end of the world.
Also we discover that the Savior in the "Our Father" has given us
an Advent prayer that is valid for all ages and for every individual: "Thy Kingdom come (*Adveniat regnum tuum*)!" It
almost looks as if this Latin word "*adveniat*" has given Advent
its name. Thus Advent itself unfolds and develops over a period of
four weeks this second petition of the Our Father.

Our deepest longing, our sincere desire, our fervent prayer
should be that the kingdom of God may grow in our hearts and in
the Church at large. May it grow "*numero et merito*," in num-
bers and in quality or depth of holiness. Like the mustard seed in
the Gospel parable, may the kingdom of God become a mighty
tree which extends to all the nations of the earth. Like the leaven,
may the kingdom of God penetrate all the areas of the Church and
our hearts.

Thus, our four-week-long prayer "*Adveniat regnum tuum*" is
a plea that this "kingdom of truth and life, this kingdom of holiness and grace, of justice, love and peace" (Preface for Feast of
Christ the King) may embrace many more hearts both in pagan
lands and in our own cities. Our "*Adveniat regnum tuum*" is a
plea that the kingdom of Christ may penetrate deeply into the
hearts of Christians and imbue and transform their whole lives.
Our "*Adveniat regnum tuum*" is a plea that the kingdom of
God might fill and sanctify with the power of its grace all Christian families, our parishes, our rectories and cloisters, countries

and people everywhere. And, finally and especially, our *"Adveniat regnum tuum"* is a plea that the kingdom of God may break into my own heart and flow and pulse through my whole being: my body, my emotions, my understanding and my will.

Let us ask the great missionary St. Francis Xavier, whose feast is celebrated at the beginning of Advent (December 3), to share with us his hunger for souls, which he expressed in his untiring prayer: *"Da mihi animas!"* Give me souls for the Kingdom of God![6]

To these words of Father Pius Parsch, we add our "Amen! Yes, Lord, Thy Kingdom come!"

* * * * * * *

CHAPTER THREE

'THE WORD BECAME FLESH'

(John 1,14)

The Christmas Celebration

THE SEASON of Advent, the period of joyful preparation and expectation for the coming of the Lord and his kingdom, gives way on the evening of December 24 to the Church's celebration of the Christmas mystery.

For most Christians, at least those of the western world, there is no more moving or more beloved celebration than that of Christmas, although it is often lamented that for many the true meaning and spirit of Christmas has been lost. In this chapter we hope to investigate and clarify the meaning and spirit of the Christmas celebration, particularly in its liturgical aspects.

The Origin and Date of the Christmas Feast in the Church

In our opening chapter on the liturgical year it was noted that Christians did not celebrate the feast of Christmas until the beginning of the fourth century. At that time there was still only the one yearly feast, that of the paschal or Easter mystery. However, at that time the tendency arose of presenting the saving action of Christ in a historical and representational way, and of distributing the celebration of the paschal mystery over a longer period and under its various aspects. For example, instead of the one Easter Vigil celebration, this was the time of the extension of the paschal celebration to include Palm Sunday, Holy Thursday, and Good Friday, each as an independent feast with its own special aspect of the paschal mystery. This tendency also led to the festal celebration of other events or mysteries of Christ's life and work, among which was the celebration of the first stage of the Christ-mystery: the incarnation and birth of Christ.[1]

A date had to be chosen for this celebration of Christ's incarnation or "becoming flesh," which mystery was seen to embrace both Christ's conception in the womb of his Mother, Mary, and his actual birth in Bethlehem. Apparently, there was no real tradition in the Church as to the actual day or date of Christ's birth; nor does the Bible present us with that information. The date that was chosen by the western Church was, we know, December 25; the Eastern Church chose January 6 for the celebration of this mystery. Later the two parts of the Church sort of swapped and adopted and adapted each other's celebration.

There is some argument as to why December 25 was chosen by the western (Roman) Church for the celebration of Christ's birth. Some maintain that the Christian theologians at that time (early fourth century) were trying to calculate the exact day of Christ's birth. Based on an earlier tradition that John the Baptist was conceived at the autumn equinox (September 25), Jesus, it was argued, would have been conceived six months later than John (the Gospels do tell us that); hence, on March 25. And, nine months from March 25 would bring us to December 25, which, at least at that time, was considered the day of the winter solstice (when the sun begins to shine longer each day in the northern hemisphere). It is said that this coincidence of Christ's birth with the winter solstice would have been considered by theologians and the Christian people in general at that time as an enchanting work of divine providence. The idea that Jesus was born into the world just on the day that the sun was being born again and overcoming the night was an idea freighted with great symbolism and one that could exalt the hearts of all.[2] Hence, according to this theory, the choice of December 25 as the date of Christ's birth was determined by the belief that Christ was actually born on this day; and, the fact that December 25 was already a pagan feast that the Church wished to christianize by instituting its own feast, was only coincidental and a minor consideration.

The stronger argument for the establishment of the feast of Christmas on December 25th is that the Church authorities did choose that day because it *was* a pagan feast to the Unconquered Sun-God (*Sol invictus*). The Roman Emperor Aurelian had established this feast on December 25th throughout the empire in A.D. 247, hoping that this feast would help unite and strengthen his vast empire. The Church of Rome, then (so this theory would hold), set up the feast of Christ's birth at least by A.D. 336, to be celebrated on the same day in order to christianize this civil celebration and to immunize Christians against the attraction of the pagan elements of the feast. Christians could then celebrate the feast of the true Sun, Christ, "the sun of justice" (Malachi 3, 20), "the light of the world" (John 8, 12), "the true light, which enlightens everyone" (John 1, 9), who alone brings light and salvation to the world.

Whatever may be the real origin for choosing December 25th as the date for our Christmas celebration, the symbolism of the "Unconquerable Sun" renewing itself and overcoming the darkness at the time of the winter solstice does contain much food for poetry and reflection in relation to Christ's birth. We will investigate this theme again in a later section when we consider the symbol of light used in the liturgy of this Christmas celebration.

The Meaning and Message of the Christmas Feast

Let us turn now to the more important consideration of just what is the meaning and message, the spirit and substance of the Christmas liturgical celebration. What should this feast mean for us today? What value and purpose does the liturgical celebration of Christ's birth have for me in my life as a Christian in this twentieth century?

There are many ways that we might attempt to answer those questions and to summarize the meaning and message of the Christmas celebration. I like the approach that Father Parsch takes when he speaks about the *three births* that we commemorate and celebrate in the Christmas liturgy. Just as there were three comings that the liturgy had in mind during the Advent season, so there are three births that are celebrated in the Christmas feast.[3]

1. The Eternal Birth of the Son from the Father

As a backdrop from which to consider Christ's birth in time, the Christmas liturgy recalls also the eternal birth of the Son of God from the Father. The child who is born in Bethlehem is the eternal Son of God, "God from God, light from light, true God from true God." There are rather frequent references to this eternal birth or begetting of the Son from the Father in the antiphons, hymns, and other prayers throughout the Christmas celebration. A few samples:

> "The eternal Word, born of the Father before time began, today emptied himself for our sake and became flesh" (Antiphon 3 of Christmas Evening Prayer).

> "You have been endowed from your birth with princely gifts; in eternal splendor, before the dawn of light on earth, I have begotten you" (Antiphon 1 of Christmas Evening Prayer II).

"Christ, born of the Father before the ages, splendor of his glory, image of his being. . ." (Petition in Morning Prayer of Dec. 31).

"Christ is your Son before all ages, yet now he is born in time" (Christmas Preface II).

"Christ, redeemer of all, the only Son of the Father, alone born from the Father before the beginning. . ." (Gregorian Christmas hymn, *"Christe, redemptor omnium"*).

Thus, as we recall the birth of the Savior at Bethlehem in time, we see that earthly or human birth from the unfathomable mystery and perspective of his birth as Son of God from the Father before time began.

2. The Human Birth of Jesus from Mary

This Son of God, born from the Father before time began, entered our time as a human child and was conceived and born from a virgin named Mary in David's town of Bethlehem. This is the second and principal birth that we recall and celebrate at Christmas. Mother Church in her liturgy takes us by the hand and leads us to the stable of Bethlehem. She shows us the newborn child, the Prince of Peace, and the Virgin-Mother rejoicing at her firstborn son. "Today is born our Savior, Christ the Lord!" (Response at Midnight Mass).

But our consideration of this birth of a child at Bethlehem must not stop at listening to or singing some Christmas carols and spending some moments before a beautifully decorated and lighted crib. The liturgy is not just celebrating the birth of a child to a young maiden in a cave or stable near Bethlehem. As we mentioned earlier, the object of the Christmas feast from the beginning embraced both the conception in the womb of Mary and the actual birth of Jesus. And so, the real mystery we are celebrating is that of the "Incarnation": the Son of God putting aside His divinity and taking on our sinful nature; the Eternal Word becoming like one of us; God with us! The child whose birth we celebrate is not just any child — he is the eternal Son of God, the promised Messiah of the ages, the firstborn of all creation, the exact representation of the Father, the mighty God, the God-man, the Emmanuel (God-with-us).

This theme of God's becoming like us, his coming to be with us and live with us in Christ, pervades the Christmas liturgy (Mass texts and the Liturgy of the Hours). But, often, I believe, we fail to meditate sufficiently on this great mystery of the Incarnation. We are satisfied with considering the historical and human details and circumstances of the birth in Bethlehem and with being stirred by the emotional feelings associated with Christmas. We need to penetrate more deeply the incarnational theme that stands out so clearly in so much of the Christmas liturgy. Again, only a sampling:

"Today, for our sake, the King of heaven chose to be born of his virgin mother. . . . All the angels cry aloud with joy, for God has come himself to save mankind" (Responsory at Office of Readings).

"In the fullness of time, chosen in the unfathomable depths of God's wisdom, the Son of God took for himself our common humanity in order to reconcile it with its creator" (Leo the Great, Second Reading of Office of Readings).

"A little child is born for us today; little and yet called the mighty God, alleluia" (Third Antiphon at Morning Prayer).

"Your eternal Word leaped down from heaven in the silent watches of the night, and now your Church is filled with wonder at the nearness of her God" (Alternative Prayer for Mass at Dawn).

"In the beginning, before time began, the Word was God; today he is born, the Savior of the world" (Third Antiphon at II Vespers).

"The Word became flesh and made his dwelling among us, and we have seen his glory, the glory of an only Son coming from the Father, filled with enduring love" (Gospel of Third Mass of Christmas).

"All this happened to fulfill what the Lord had said through the prophet: 'The virgin shall be with child and give birth to a son, and they shall call him Emmanuel,' a name which means 'God is with us!' " (Gospel of Christmas Vigil Mass).

It is, therefore, the great mystery of the Incarnation, God coming to be with us in the most perfect way possible by taking on our very nature and existence — that is the deepest meaning of the birth in Bethlehem that we celebrate. It is because this child is God-become-flesh that his birth means the beginning of our salvation. His birth issues in the fullness of time when God will restore and reconcile all things to himself.

3. Our Birth as Children of God

That brings us to the third birth that the Christmas liturgy celebrates: Christ's birth in us, or our birth (rebirth) in Christ! The only Son of God has become a human being; he was born in order to make us his brothers and sisters and heirs with him of eternal life. Christ became a child of earth so that we might become children of heaven, so that we might be born again as sons and daughters of God.

Pope St. Leo in one of his Christmas homilies (Office of Readings for December 31) speaks clearly and beautifully of this birth of Christ in us at the Christmas celebration:

In the very act in which we are reverencing the birth of our Savior, we are also celebrating our own new birth. For the birth of Christ is the origin of the Christian people; and the birthday of the head is also the birthday of the body.

Though each and every individual occupies a definite place in this body to which he has been called, and though all the progeny of the Church is differentiated and marked with the passage of time, nevertheless as the whole community of the faithful, once begotten in the baptismal font, was crucified with Christ in the passion, raised up with him in the resurrection, and at the ascension placed at the right hand of the Father, so too it is born with him in the Nativity, which we are celebrating today. For every believer regenerated in Christ, no matter in what part of the the whole world he may be, breaks with that ancient way of life that derives from original sin, and by rebirth is transformed into a new person. Henceforth that person is reckoned to be the stock, not of his earthly father, but of Christ, who became Son of Man precisely that we could become children of God; for unless in humility he had come down to us, none of us by our own merits could ever go up to him.

This theme of Christ being born so that we might be reborn, of his becoming a human child sharing our nature so that we might become children of God sharing the divine nature, is frequently called "the holy or marvelous exchange." The Fathers of the Church frequently develop this theme of the "holy exchange" in their writings on the incarnation and birth of Christ, and abundant references to this theme are found throughout the liturgy of the Christmas season. The Third Preface for Christmas is taken up almost entirely with this theme: "Today in him (Christ) a new light has dawned upon the world: God has become one with man, and man has become one again with God. Your eternal Word has taken upon himself our human weakness, giving our mortal nature immortal value. So marvelous is this oneness between God and man that in Christ man restores to man the gift of everlasting life." Or again, the first antiphon for Vespers on January 1 announces: "O marvelous exchange! Man's Creator has become man, born of a virgin. We have been made sharers in the divinity of Christ who humbled himself to share in our humanity.''

This "holy exchange" theme sums up in some ways the three births that the liturgy celebrates at Christmas: the Son of God, born from the Father before time began, becomes a human child and subject to all our human experiences and imperfections except sin so that we can become children of God; he is born for us so that we can be reborn in him.

So, Christmas is also the day of our rebirth in Christ and his birth in us. It's true that the Easter Vigil is the special annual celebration of our baptism and rebirth in Christ; but, if we have been longing and praying for the coming of Christ and his kingdom to us in all its fullness during the weeks of Advent, then Christ will indeed be born again in us in the liturgy of Christmas day. Bethlehem will be the town or city in which we are attending Mass; the stable will be the church in which we are gathered; and our own hearts will be the manger in which the eternal Word of God becomes flesh again, making us sharers in his eternal, divine life. Then we can truly and humbly say: "Today is born our Savior, Christ the Lord!''

The Three Masses of Christmas

Since the sixth century every priest was permitted to celebrate three Masses on Christmas, which custom continues in our day. There are special Mass texts and readings for a midnight Mass, a Mass at dawn, and a Mass during the day.

The origin of these three Masses is of historical nature and developed in Rome. At first, in the fourth century, there was only one Mass, celebrated by the Pope at St. Peter's in the morning about nine o'clock. Then in the fifth century, the midnight Mass and an early morning Mass were added in imitation of the Jerusalem Christians, who were already celebrating Mass at two different times on Christmas. The Jerusalem Christians would celebrate a midnight Mass in the Church which Emperor Constantine had built over the cave of Christ's birth in Bethlehem; then they would return in procession to Jerusalem and celebrate another Mass in the early morning there. In Rome the midnight Mass was celebrated in the Crib Church of St. Mary Major; the second Mass, in the Church of the Resurrection of St. Anastasius; and the third Mass, in St. Peter's. From Rome the custom of the three Masses on Christmas spread throughout the western Church.[4]

Some of the medieval mystics tried to see in these three Christmas Masses an allusion to the "threefold birth" of Christ that we spoke of in our previous section of this chapter. Adolf Adam quotes one of these mystics, John Tauler, who made that connection in this way:

> The first and supreme birth takes place when the heavenly Father bears his only-begotten Son as one with himself in essence yet as also a distinct person. The second birth, which we commemorate today, results from the maternal fruitfulness which the chaste Virgin exercised in perfect purity. The third birth is this: that God is truly but spiritually born every day and at every hour in a good soul, as a result of grace and love. We celebrate these three births by means of the three holy Masses.[5]

Rather than the celebration of three births of Christ in these three Masses of Christmas, the three liturgies are based more on the accord of the event described in the Gospel of each Mass with the time of the celebration and on the light-symbolism of the times of celebration. The Gospel for the midnight Mass, for example, relates the events that took place at night when the angel appeared to the shepherds "keeping night-watch." The child who is born at night is the great light that has appeared to the "people who walked in darkness" (First Reading); "the splendor of Jesus Christ our light" makes this holy night radiant (Opening Prayer).

In the Mass at dawn, the Gospel tells of the shepherds coming to visit the Christ-child, presumably in the early morning as the sun is rising. The Opening Prayer reflects the time of sunrise as the priest prays: "Father, we are filled with the new light by the coming of your Word among us. May the light of faith shine in our words and actions." And in the Responsorial Verse and Psalm we sing: "A light will shine on us today"; "light dawns for the just, and gladness for the upright of heart."

The third Mass is celebrated in the full light of day, and many of the texts of this Mass During the Day seem to reflect this full light of day:

> "All the ends of the earth have seen the saving power of God" (Responsory after First Reading).
>
> "This son is the reflection of the Father's glory" (Second Reading).
>
> "Today a great light has come upon the earth" (Alleluia Verse).
>
> "The light shines on in darkness, a darkness that did not overcome it. . . . We have seen his glory, the glory of an only Son coming from the Father" (Gospel).

Our Christmas feast is indeed a feast of the Sol Invictus, the Unconquerable Sun!

The Other Feasts Connected with Christmas

The "twelve days of Christmas" from December 25 to January 6 continue the celebration of Christ's coming into the world and consider this great mystery from various aspects, with emphasis on different elements of the mystery of God-become-flesh.

1. December 26, 27, 28: Feasts of St. Stephen, St. John the Evangelist, and the Holy Innocents

On the three days immediately after Christmas, we have

the feasts of St. Stephen, the first martyr of the Church; St. John, the Apostle and Evangelist; and the Holy Innocents. Although there is no actual relationship between the first two feasts and their placement on these days immediately after the birth of Christ (they were celebrated on these days before the feast of Christmas was instituted), the liturgy does endeavor to relate them in some way to the feast of Christmas.

The three feasts taken together are seen as presenting us with companions of the newborn King and of the King who is to come. Stephen, John, and the Holy Innocents (the first martyr, a virgin beloved of Christ, and virgin-martyrs) are representatives of those 144,000 who follow the Lamb wherever he goes, as described in the Book of Revelation. They are those "who were not defiled . . . and these are the ones who follow the Lamb wherever he goes . . . they have been ransomed as the first fruits of the human race for God and the Lamb" (Revelation 14, 4).

The relationship of St. Stephen's martyrdom with Christmas is brought out clearly in the Second Reading of the Office of Readings, where St. Fulgentius of Ruspe writes: "Yesterday we celebrated the birth in time of our eternal King. Today we celebrate the triumphant suffering of his soldier. Yesterday our king, clothed in his robe of flesh, left his place in the virgin's womb and graciously visited the world. Today his soldier leaves the tabernacle of his body and goes triumphantly to heaven."

The liturgy is not so explicit in relating the feast of St. John the Evangelist to the Christmas celebration, although John is presented above all in the liturgical texts as the one who has given witness to the Word of God who became flesh and whom John had seen.

The feast of the Holy Innocents is, of course, more directly related to the birth of Christ, since Herod was trying to kill the Christ-child in his murdering of these small children in Bethlehem. St. Quodvultdeus, in a sermon used in the Second Reading of the Office of Readings for this feast, spells out movingly this relation between Christ and the Holy Innocents: "The children die for Christ, though they do not know it. The parents mourn for the death of martyrs. The child [Christ] makes of these yet unable to speak fit witnesses of himself. See the kind of kingdom that is his, coming as he did in order to be this kind of king. See how the deliverer is already working deliverance, the savior already working salvation."

2. The Feast of the Holy Family

The Feast of the Holy Family, celebrated on the Sunday within the Octave of Christmas, is also easily related to the Christmas mystery, although its origin is only from the late nineteenth century and has no direct, historical connection with the Christmas celebration. The feast, a so-called "idea feast," focuses on the fact that the Son-of-God-become-flesh lived among us as a member of a human family in order to give us a model of perfect family life in Jesus, Mary, and Joseph. "In history's moment when all was ready, you sent your Son to dwell in time, obedient to the laws of life in our world. Teach us the sanctity of human love, show us the value of family life, and help us to live in peace with all men and women that we may share in your life for ever" (Alternate Opening Prayer).

3. January 1, the Solemnity of Mary, the Mother of God

On the octave day of Christmas, the liturgy brings us back as it were to the stable at Bethlehem. But this time our focus is on the woman from whom this Son of God was born (Second Reading); namely, the Virgin Mary, who "treasured all these things and reflected on them in her heart" (Gospel Reading). St. Athanasius points out in the Second Reading of the Office of Readings for this solemnity how this birth from Mary is so closely related to the true humanness of Christ and the mystery of God-with-us: "What was born of Mary was therefore human by nature, in accordance with the inspired Scriptures, and the body of the Lord was a true body. It was a true body because it was the same as ours. Mary, you see, is our sister, for we are all born from Adam."

This feast in honor of Mary, the Mother of God, is perhaps one of the oldest feasts in honor of Mary. It was probably originally placed on January 1 to offset the Roman pagan celebrations of the New Year on this day. (Julius Caesar shifted the beginning of the new year from March 1 to January 1 in 46 B.C.. Later, January 1 became the Feast of the Circumcision of our Lord, and the octave day of Christmas; but the reform of the liturgy after the Second Vatican Council reinstated this feast as the Solemnity of Mary, the Mother of God. "O Mary, your blessed and fruitful virginity is like the bush, flaming yet unburned, which Moses saw on Sinai. Pray for us, Mother of God" (Antiphon 3 of Vespers II).

4. The Feast of Epiphany

The twelve days of solemn celebration of the Christmas mystery close with the Solemnity of the Epiphany of the Lord on January 6, or in some countries on the Second Sunday after Christmas.

This Feast of the Epiphany, as we mentioned at the outset of this chapter, was the original feast of Christ's birth in the Eastern Church. The choice of the date, January 6, was probably influenced, like that of December 25, by a pagan feast celebrated on that day in the East. This pagan feast was that of the birthday of the god Arion (god of time and eternity).

The word "epiphany" is a Greek word which means "revelation," "appearance," or "manifestation." The chief appearance or manifestation that this feast celebrates is the manifestation of the God-man to the wise men from the East who, led by the star, come to recognize and adore the newborn King of heaven and earth.

The other revelations or manifestations of Christ that are recalled in the Feast of the Epiphany are Christ's changing of water into wine at the wedding feast of Cana, where he "*re-*

vealed his glory, and his disciples began to believe in him" (John 2, 11), and the baptism of Jesus by John, when the heavens are opened and the voice reveals or makes manifest that this Jesus is the beloved Son of God. Traces of these two appearances or manifestations are still found in some of the ancient texts used in this feast (e.g., the Antiphon for the Canticle of Mary of Vespers II and several of the Second Readings of the Office of Readings during the days after this feast).

The chief event that we celebrate on this Solemnity of the Epiphany of the Lord is, however, the visit and adoration of the Lord by the Magi or wise men from the East. (The belief that they were "kings" and that there were "three" of them comes from the reference in the Scriptures that they offered the *three* gifts of gold, incense, and myrrh and from Psalm 72 which is used in this feast and proclaims in one of its verses: "The *kings* of Arabia and Seba shall bring tribute. All kings shall pay him homage, all nations shall serve him.")

The central theme that this Feast of Epiphany proclaims is that this child born in Bethlehem is the *Savior and King of all peoples and nations*. The appearance of the star that guided the Magi to Christ, the dove and the voice speaking from the cloud at Jesus' baptism, and the changing of water into wine at Cana are all manifestations that this Jesus, son of Mary, is also Son of God. On Christmas day we focus our attention more on the fact that God has appeared as a human being and dwelt among us; on Epiphany, we focus on the fact that this Jesus, born of Mary, manifested himself to the whole world as God. Explains Father Parsch: "*Weihnacht ist das Fest der Menschwerdung, der Menscherscheinung; Epiphanie das Fest der Gotterscheinung Christi.* [Christmas is the feast of Christ's becoming and appearing as a human being; Epiphany is the feast of Christ's appearing as God]."

Since the word "epiphany" means "appearance, revelation, manifestation," we might expect that the symbol of light will also be very prominent in this feast. We are not disappointed.

The "light of the star" that led the Magi to Christ is seen as a symbol of the "light of faith" that leads us to heaven (Opening Prayer, Communion Prayer, and Final Blessing). Also, Christ is portrayed as the "light of all peoples" in the Preface for Epiphany and in many other of the liturgical texts for this feast. Let this one example from the Liturgy of the Hours suffice to illustrate the role of the light-symbol in this feast:

> "Jerusalem, your light has come;
> the glory of the Lord dawns upon you.
> Men of every race shall walk in the splendor of your sunrise, alleluia" (Antiphon 3 of Morning Prayer).

What the Christmas Celebration Demands of Us

We close this chapter on the Christmas celebration by focusing more directly on what the liturgy of this Christmas period asks and demands of us as our response to the birth of Christ. During this time we meet and encounter Christ, and this encounter with the God-made-flesh should produce a response and a change in us.

God has come into our world, as we mentioned earlier in the section on the three "births" of Christ at Christmas, precisely so that we might become the children of God. He came down to us so that we might ascend to him. He took on our human nature so that we might share in his divine nature. The basic moral demand, then, of this Christmas celebration would be that we put off the things of the flesh and the world and seek more after the things of God, walking as children of light. Pope St. Leo the Great, in the sermon for Christmas used as the Second Reading in the Office of Readings, put that moral demand this way:

> Let us throw off our old nature and all its ways and, as we have come to birth in Christ, let us renounce the works of the flesh. Christian, remember your dignity, and now that you share in God's own nature, do not return by sin to your former base condi-

tion. Bear in mind who is your head and of whose body you are a member. Do not forget that you have been rescued from the power of darkness and brought into the light of God's kingdom.

The passage from Chapter Two of Titus (11-12), which is used in the Liturgy of the Hours and also as the Second Reading for the midnight Mass of Christmas, echoes to a certain extent the challenge of St. Leo: "The grace of God has appeared, offering salvation to all. It trains us to reject godless ways and worldly desires, and to live temperately, justly, and devoutly in this age."

Besides this general call to reject the values of the sinful world and to be children of light, the liturgies throughout Christmastide do not really call us to the practice of any specific virtues, not even that of giving and generosity toward others. There is, however, an indirect though consistent call for us to become more appreciative of God's great love and gift to us of his Son; to become more aware of God's presence in our world and to see the Word-made-flesh reflected in those whose lives we touch; also, to become joyful heralds and lights of Christ's Gospel of peace and love by more fully living the peace and love that has been given us through Christ.

It almost seems, to me at least, that the Church's liturgy of the Christmas period does not issue us a ringing moral challenge, but is content if we but meditate deeply during this time on the mystery of the Incarnation of Christ, much like Mary, who "kept all these things, reflecting on them in her heart" (Luke 2, 19). Such consistent reflection and meditation will then serve to deepen and strengthen the basic appreciation and faith that we have in God's presence and love. This enkindled faith will overflow simply and abundantly in lives of holiness and goodness. It is as if the Word of God must become flesh in our minds and hearts before he becomes flesh in the words and actions of our daily lives.

53

"The Word [of God] became flesh
and made his dwelling among us. . . .
From his fullness we have all received. . . ." (John 1, 14, 16).

* * * * * * *

CHAPTER FOUR

'THE DAY ... CALLED THE LORD'S DAY'

(Constitution on the Liturgy, n. 106)

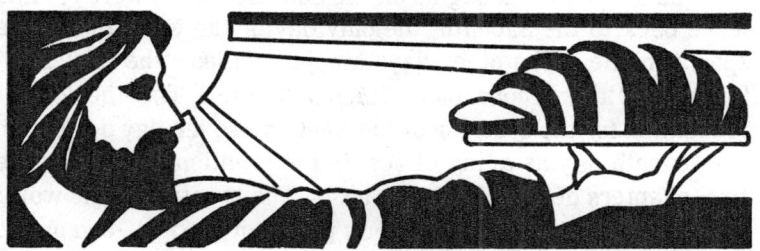

The Sunday Celebration and Sundays of Ordinary Time

"THE SUNDAY CELEBRATION . . . the 'weekly Easter' is the core of our spiritual and liturgical lives, the center around which all of our prayer and activity must revolve."[1] These words of a noted theologian and Bible scholar bring out the importance of the Sunday celebration for each of us as the followers of Christ. The Sunday celebration is the core, the center, the heart of our lives as Christians. All of our other prayers and all the other activities, religious and otherwise, must revolve around the Sunday celebration of the Eucharist. *The Constitution on the Liturgy* of Vatican II expressed that same truth in these words: "The Sunday . . . is the foundation and kernel of the whole liturgical year."[2]

In this chapter we wish to review the development of the Sunday celebration in the history of the Church and to examine the various motives for celebrating Sunday with faith and enthusiasm and joy so that it may truly become the foundation and center of our lives.

The Jewish Week and the Sabbath

We might begin by recalling some of the essentials of the Jewish week as it was known and lived by the apostles and the early Judeo-Christians.

The Jewish week begins on the Sabbath (our Saturday) and leads back to the Sabbath, the only day of the week that has a special name. (The other days are just called "the first day" [Sunday], "the second day" [Monday], etc.) The theological foundation for the ordering of the week in a seven-day cycle with the seventh day as a day of rest is the creation account in the first chapters of the Book of Genesis. The creation of the world is described as taking place over a period of six days, and on the seventh day "God rested . . . from all the work he had undertaken. So God blessed the seventh day and made it holy. . ." (Genesis 2, 2-3).

Thus, the Sabbath was to be a day holy to the Jewish people — a day of thanksgiving and prayer, a day of special communion with the Lord of creation, a day of rest from work and other ordinary activities in imitation of God's rest.

The Christian Observance of Sunday

It was the "first day" of the Jewish week (our Sunday) that became the most important day of celebration for the first Christians and the first component of a liturgical year. The first Christians considered this day to play a most essential role in the history of salvation, for it was on this day that the Lord rose from the dead as all the evangelists agree (cf. Matthew 28, 1 ff; Mark 16, 1 ff; Luke 24, 13ff; John 20, 1 ff). It was also the day the Lord seemed to prefer for his appearances to the disciples (Matthew 28, 9; Luke 24, 13 ff; John 20, 19ff), and it was the day on which Jesus sent his promised Spirit on the Apostles in the form of fiery tongues, sending them forth to bring the good news to the world. This "first day of the week" became for the early Christians "the day the Lord has made" (Psalm 118, 24) and soon they gave it the name "the Lord's Day."

The first Judeo-Christians continued to attend the synagogue on the Sabbath, so their celebration on Sunday was not just a substitution for the Sabbath observance, at least not in the early years of Christianity. But on Sunday the Christians would gather together in the evening (the hour of the principal meal) or in the early morning "to break bread," as we read in the Acts of the Apostles (20, 7). The times of early morning or the evening were chosen because the Sunday was a day of work like any other, and those were the only times that the Christians could assemble. This was the situation for the first three centuries of Christianity.

The essential element of their gathering together was to celebrate "the Lord's Supper," the Mass or Eucharist. There was no uniform ritual for the various churches in the apostolic times, and various other elements such as Scripture readings, prophecies, speaking in tongues and their interpretation, hymns and the *agapé* (love-feast) were joined to the breaking of the bread in memory of the Lord's resurrection and his continuing presence in their midst.

The Importance of the Sunday Observance
for the Early Church

The observance of Sunday as a special day of worship for the Christians through their gathering together "to break bread" was considered of greatest importance by them. Though there did not exist a positive commandment or precept of the Church declaring attendance at the Sunday gathering a strict duty (this did not come until the Lateran Council in 1215), some of the earliest Christian documents that we have do have warnings and exhortations regarding the Sunday observance. For example, in the Letter to the Hebrews we find this exhortation: "Let us hold unwaveringly to our confession that gives us hope . . . not stay away from our assembly, as is the custom of some" (10, 23-25). The "Didache" (*The Teaching of the Twelve Apostles*), one of the earliest Christian catechetical documents, speaks of the duty of attending the Sunday Eucharist in these words: "Assemble on the Lord's Day, break bread and give thanks after you have first confessed your sins so that your sacrifice may be pure." And Ignatius of Antioch, a bishop of the early Church, makes the celebration of the Sunday a badge of identification for Christians. Just as Christians were to be known by the love they show to one another, so were they to be identified by their gathering together on Sunday to worship the Lord and celebrate the Eucharist in his memory.

In his book on the liturgical year, Adolf Adam quotes a Christian document of the mid-third century (*Didascalia of the Apostles*) which brings out quite strikingly the importance and necessity that the Christians in that age of martyrs attached to the celebration of the Eucharist on Sunday:

> Since therefore you are the members of Christ, do not scatter yourselves from the Church by not assembling. Seeing that you have Christ for your head, who as he promised is present and in communion with you, be not then neglectful of yourselves, and deprive not our Savior of his members, and do not rend and scatter his body; and make not your worldly affairs of more account than the word of God. But on the Lord's day leave everything and run eagerly to your Church, for she is your glory. Otherwise, what excuse have they before God who do not assemble on the Lord's day to hear the word of life and be nourished by the divine food which abides forever?

St. John Chrysostom, writing in the fourth century on the Christians' unceasing custom of assembling for the Eucharist, said: "This meal is a meal of brotherly union, for all take part in it as in the Lord himself. To abstain from this meal is to separate oneself from the Lord: the Sunday meal is that which we take in common with the Lord and with the brethren."[3]

Hence, when we study this whole history of the early Church and its coming together to celebrate the Eucharist on "the first day of the week," we see that the observance of this celebration on the Lord's Day of Resurrection is not a mere canonical regulation which might be repealed by the Church authorities. No, it is an observance that goes back to that very "first day of the week," the first Christian Sunday, when Jesus rose from the dead and walked with the disciples on the road to Emmaus and broke bread with them and later stood in the midst of the apostles in the Upper Room, eating with them and bestowing his spirit on them. That "first day of the week" was henceforth to be devoted by Christians to gathering together with one another and with Christ as the apostles had done on the first Easter Day, recalling and celebrating his death and resurrection and his continued presence in their midst until he comes again on the last day.

The Early Christian Names for Sunday

The significance and importance attached to Sunday by the early Christians can also be gleaned from the various names they gave to this day.

1. "First Day of the Week"

We have already mentioned that at first the Christians spoke of Sunday as "the first day of the week" following Jewish custom. But, since according to the Genesis account of creation the light was created on the first day and separated from the darkness, soon the Christian writers began to connect this "day of light" with the "new creation" accomplished by Christ's resurrection. Christ is the new light that has overcome the darkness and "which enlightens everyone" (John 1, 9).

2. "The Lord's Day"

We have also referred to a new expression that soon came into use among the Christians for Sunday. It was the expression "the Lord's Day" (*"kuriaké"* in Greek, *"dominica"* in Latin). The Apocalypse or Book of Revelation already made use of this expression when the author introduced his visions by saying he was "caught up in spirit on the Lord's day" (Revelation 1, 10). The "Lord" of course is one of the titles for Jesus, especially for the risen and glorified Jesus; and it was on this first day of the week that God made his Son "both Lord and Messiah, this Jesus whom you crucified" (Acts 2, 36). "The Lord's Day" was thus to be a remembrance of the resurrection of the Lord and a celebration of "the Lord's supper" (1 Corinthians 11, 20) at which the Christians assembled to be with their risen Lord.

The Romance languages which derived from Latin still preserve this expression "the Lord's Day" in their terminology for Sunday: *"domenica"* (Italian), *"domingo"* (Spanish), *"dimanche"* (French).

3. "The Eighth Day"

Another expression used by the early Christians for the Sunday was "the eighth day," a name little used anymore today, although the *Constitution on the Liturgy* of Vatican II mentions that "the Church celebrates the paschal mystery every eighth day, which day is appropriately called the Lord's Day on Sunday" (n. 106).

Why call "the first day of the week" also "the eighth day"? Justin Martyr, an early Christian apologist, explained: "Sunday is the first day of the week, but it is also numbered as the eighth day when it returns at the end of the weekly cycle; yet it does not cease to be the first." To call Sunday "the eighth day" (*"Ogdoad"* in Greek) is simply putting the emphasis on the new creation that began on this day, a creation that is eternal and will never end. The "eighth day" represents the eternity of God and the eternity shared by mankind redeemed by the death and resurrection of Christ. "The day of the Lord," declared St. Augustine, "as an eternal octave, consecrated by the resurrection of Christ, prefigures eternal rest. . . . What is our end, if it is not to arrive at the kingdom without end?"

4. "The Day of the Lord's Resurrection"

Another name which was used by Tertullian at the beginning of the third century and by later Christian Greek writers was "the day of the Lord's Resurrection" or "Resurrection Day." The name for Sunday in many Slavic languages has this meaning, which makes clear that Sunday is the weekly celebration of Christ's passover from death to new life.

5. The Name "Sunday"

We should add that the name "Sunday" or "day of the Sun" did not have a Christian origin, but began in the Greco-Roman world and then came to us in English through the Germanic languages. The Greco-Roman world had a planetary week in which the days of the week were named after the planets. Among the planets were included the sun and the moon, since the earth was considered the center of the universe. Sunday was, hence, the "Day of the Sun"; Monday, the "day of the Moon"; and Tuesday through Saturday were named after the planets Mars, Mercury, Jupiter, Venus, and Saturn. (Our English names for these days come from the Anglo-Saxon words for these planets or gods: Tiw, Woden, Thor, Freo, and Saeter.)

At first the Christians did not wish to make use of the expression "day of the Sun" for the first day of the week, because the name was associated with pagan astrology and worship of the Sun as a god. Gradually, however, when the name "Sunday" became widespread throughout the Roman empire, the Church accepted the name but gave a Christian interpretation to it, seeing the sun as a symbol of the Risen Christ, the "sun that never sets." St. Jerome, who wrote toward the end of the fourth century, provides the classic Christian interpretation of the "day of the Sun," as well as that of the more preferred expression, "the Lord's Day":

> The Lord's day, the day of the resurrection, the day of Christians: that is our day. It is called the Lord's day because on it the Lord ascended victoriously to the Father. When pagans speak of it as the day of the sun, we gladly agree, for on this day the light of the world, the sun of justice, arose and salvation is hidden in the shelter of his wings.

The Prohibition of Work on Sunday

One of the features that many Catholics, especially older Catholics, associate with the observance of Sunday is the prohibition of work on Sunday. It may surprise many that this prohibition of work on Sunday is not at all an original feature of the Christian Sunday observance.

One of the only prohibitive features of the early Christian observance of Sunday was not work, but the prohibition of kneeling for prayer and of fasting on Sunday! This prohibition, which applied also to the fifty days of Eastertide (when that season developed), was to be a sign of joy for the Christian. To pray kneeling and to fast were signs of penitence and sorrow, but to pray standing was a sign of fervor and joy in recognition of the Christian's sharing in the resurrection and glory of Jesus.

We have noted earlier that Sundays were not holidays but ordinary workdays for the first Christians, and so they had to assemble for the Lord's Supper in the early morning or in the evening after the workday was over. So for several centuries there was no connection between the Sunday observance and the prohibition from work as the Jewish sabbath demanded.

When the Roman Emperor Constantine became a Christian in the fourth century, he had a law passed in A.D. 321 that proclaimed "the venerable day of the sun" was to be a day of rest for all judges and for city and business people. The farmers, however, could continue to work on Sunday and the slaves were also allowed to work and hence were exempt from the law of Sunday rest. These edicts of Constantine were an important step in the development of the Sunday observance because they made it easier for the Christians to celebrate the Sunday liturgy, as well as to have the opportunity for welfare work and for relaxation of mind and body.

Gradually, however, Sunday as a "day of rest" became more important than Sunday as a "day of worship." By the end of the sixth century, agricultural work and all "servile work" (the work of slaves, i.e., hard manual labor) was forbidden, and not only that work that was incompatible with the divine worship to be carried out on Sundays. Such "servile work" on Sunday came to be considered a serious violation of both Church and civil law and was dealt with by even harsher punishments. The Council of Narbonne (589), for example, passed this decree: "If anyone dares to do this [work on Sunday] he shall, if he is a freeman, pay the city judge six pieces of gold; if he is a serf, he shall receive a hundred lashes."

With this emphasis on Sunday as a "day of rest," there were some appeals by the Christian writers and preachers to the Old Testament sabbath laws. But generally the official Church and most Christian writers made it clear that the sabbath laws were part of Jewish ceremonial law and did not bind Christians. The impression was certainly given, however, that the Sunday rest was a continuation of the Jewish sabbath, just on a different day of the week. And for many centuries very great attention was given to the prohibition of work on Sundays, especially in moral theology textbooks. The sad result was that the Christological meaning of Sunday as a celebration of the Lord's resurrection and his presence in the midst of his people was obscured — and probably still is — in the minds of many Christians.

The Christian Observance of Sunday
in the Twentieth Century

What of the Christian observance of Sunday in our world of

the twentieth century? I would like to answer that question first with the entire text of n. 106 of the *Constitution on the Sacred Liturgy* of the Second Vatican Council. This paragraph brings out quite well, I believe, the importance of the observance of Sunday as a "day of worship" and also as a "day of rest" as well as the Christological significance of this first day of the week:

> By a tradition handed down from the apostles which took its origin from the very day of Christ's resurrection, the Church celebrates the paschal mystery every eighth day; with good reason this, then, bears the name of the Lord's day or Sunday. For on this day Christ's faithful should come together into one place so that, by hearing the word of God and taking part in the Eucharist, they may call to mind the passion, the resurrection, and the glorification of the Lord Jesus, and may thank God who 'has begotten them again, through the resurrection of Jesus Christ from the dead, unto a living hope" (1 Peter 1, 3). Hence the Lord's day is the original feast day, and it should be proposed to the piety of the faithful and taught to them so that it may become in fact a day of joy and of freedom from work. Other celebrations, unless they truly be of greatest importance, shall not have precedence over the Sunday which is the foundation and kernel of the whole liturgical year.

Adolf Adam in his book *The Liturgical Year*, written originally in German, presents some excerpts from The Joint Synod of the Dioceses of the Federal Republic of Germany, which explored the ideas presented by Vatican II regarding Sunday and gave them more concrete application. I would like to summarize what I consider the more important of these observations and applications of the German synod:

> 1. The weekly Christian celebration is essentially a "sign" of the salvific reality of the new creation that began with the resurrection of Christ.

> 2. As a feast of the Christian community, a day of eucharistic

celebration, and a day of Christian anticipation of what is to come, Sunday is *indispensable*, and no other day of the week can substitute for it.

3. Some important *functions* of Sunday for the people of our day are: strengthening their faith, fitting them for worship and for service in the world, liberating them from the many pressures of a way of life that is determined by industrial mass-society, and preventing their enslavement and isolation by the world of work.

4. Sunday can once again become a *real festive day* if our actions bring relaxation and joy while also fostering leisure and meditation through dialogue with one another, play, and other shared activities.

5. All the faithful have a *serious duty* of regularly taking part in the Sunday liturgy as an expression of gratitude and love for God and of responsibility to themselves and to the community, and also in order to represent and make up for those who absent themselves from the liturgy or do not yet know the Lord.

6. We should not forget that Sunday is not a day of rest for many people, such as working mothers, employees in service jobs, and health-care personnel in homes and hospitals. Christians are challenged, in view of the traditional connection of visiting relatives and the sick and lonely on Sunday, to help carry their neighbor's burden by generously enabling such people mentioned above to have a free Sunday or a few free hours by substituting for them on Sunday.

The Sundays of Ordinary Time

We wish to conclude this chapter on the Sunday celebration by saying a few words about the Sundays of Ordinary Time in the liturgical year.

In the structure of the present liturgical year, besides the two great cycles of Christmas and Easter, there is the temporal cycle or Ordinary Time of the Year, which is essential to the liturgical year. This temporal cycle is divided into two parts: the

Sundays after the Feast of the Baptism of the Lord until Lent begins, and the Sundays after Pentecost until the Christmas Cycle begins with the First Sunday of Advent. In all there are thirty-three or thirty-four weeks in this "Ordinary Time."

What is the character of these Sundays of Ordinary Time? A famous liturgist, Jounel, said this of these Sundays: "They are Sundays in a pure state. They have no secondary traits but simply embody the very essence of the Christian Sunday or Lord's Day as presented to us in the tradition of the Church. Each of them is an Easter, each a feast."

Each of the Sundays of Ordinary Time now has its own prayers and readings. The readings are in a three-year cycle and there are three readings assigned for each Sunday: a selection from the Old Testament, a passage from the Letters of Paul or James or Hebrews, and a Gospel selection from Matthew in Year A, Mark in Year B and Luke in Year C.

The Old Testament reading chosen for the Sundays of Ordinary Time has been chosen with the theme of the Gospel in mind, and so we should look for a common theme in those two readings. The second readings, however, are simply semi-continuous passages from a particular New Testament Letter, and only coincidentally might have a common theme with the First Reading and the Gospel selection. Too often, it seems to me, homiletic preparation materials try to force the ideas of the second reading into a common theme with the first reading and the Gospel passage for the day.

Finally, we should add that there are certain feasts of the Lord that occur during Ordinary Time. Those that occur on Sundays are: the Solemnity of the Trinity (first Sunday after Pentecost); the Solemnity of the Body and Blood of Christ or Corpus Christi (second Sunday after Pentecost in our country); and the Solemnity of Christ the King (the last Sunday of Ordinary Time).

* * * * * * *

CHAPTER FIVE

'TURN TO ME AND LIVE'

(Ezekiel 33, 11)

The Lenten Season

THE FIRST GREAT cycle of the liturgical year, the Christmas Cycle (First Sunday of Advent to the Feast of the Baptism of the Lord), centered on the mystery of the Incarnation of Christ, his coming into the world as a human being. The second great cycle of the liturgical year, the Easter Cycle, deals with another great mystery of our faith: the salvation or redemption of the world brought about by the God-become-flesh through his sufferings, death, and resurrection from the dead.

As we have seen in Chapters Two and Three, the theme of "light" played an important role in the liturgy of the whole Christmas Cycle. Christ was the "light from light," the splendor of the Father who came into the world to dispel the darkness of sin and to enable us to become "children of light." Indeed, we might characterize and summarize the Christmas liturgy in the phrase: CHRIST THE LIGHT OF THE WORLD!

Although there is a trace of the theme of light in the Easter Cycle (e.g., the darkness fights against the light but does not overcome it; "Christ our light" of the Easter Vigil, etc.), the more prominent symbol and theme in the Easter Cycle is that of "life": CHRIST THE LIFE OF THE WORLD! (The two cycles together: "the light of life" [John 8, 12].) Christ is the life of the world, who through his suffering and dying conquered sin and death and now lives eternally. And he shares that resurrected life with us in the sacraments, especially the sacraments of baptism and the Holy Eucharist. "Through death to life" is another phrase that captures well the central mystery and meaning of the cycle.

The Parts of the Easter Cycle

Before the extensive liturgical reforms of the Second Vatican Council, the Easter Cycle of the Church year began with a three-week pre-Lenten season (the weeks of Septuagesima, Sexagesima and Quinquagesima). Next came Lent proper, beginning with Ash Wednesday and ending with a special period called "Passiontide" (the two weeks before Easter) up to noon of Holy Saturday. Then, after the seven weeks of the Easter celebration, there followed the twenty-four Sundays after Pentecost, a period considered loosely as part of the Easter Cycle.

The reform of the liturgical year springing from the Second Vatican Council has streamlined the Easter Cycle to some extent. There exists no longer a pre-Lenten season; the Easter Cycle begins with the first day of Lent, Ash Wednesday. "Passiontide" has also been eliminated and the period of Lent covers approximately forty days and officially ends at the celebration of the Lord's Supper on Holy Thursday. Holy Thursday, Good Friday, and Holy Saturday are called the "Easter Triduum," ("the holy Three Days of Easter") and are considered as one unified celebration of the Easter or paschal mystery as in the earlier Church. The final part of the Easter Cycle is the period of fifty days after Easter Sunday until Pentecost, which feast now brings the Easter Cycle to a close.

We will have three chapters that deal with this complete Easter Cycle. The present chapter will treat of Lent, the forty-day period of preparation; Chapter Six will center in on Holy Week and the Easter Triduum; and Chapter Seven will deal with the rest of the Easter Cycle to Pentecost.

The Historical Development of Lent

As we have already mentioned in Chapter One, there were no cycles or seasons of the liturgical year in the early Church, although at a very early period there was an annual commemoration of the Pasch or Easter Feast. As a preparation for this Easter Feast there was observed in some places during the first three centuries of the Church a preparation of only forty consecutive hours or a couple of days or a week at the most.

The fourth century, however, saw the development of the Easter Triduum (Holy Thursday, Good Friday, Holy Saturday) and also the forty-day period of preparation for Easter, so that by the end of this century the forty-day period of fast was being observed everywhere in both East and West.

The origin of this preparation period most probably came from the custom of an intensive period of preparation of adult candidates for baptism, which sacrament was received during the Easter Vigil. The number "forty" was undoubtedly based on the Lord's forty-day fast in the desert after his baptism in the Jordan; but the Church Fathers also saw in this practice an echo of the forty-day fast of Moses on Mt. Sinai before receiving the Ten Commandments (Exodus 34, 28), the forty-day fast of the prophet Elijah on his journey to Mt. Horeb (1 Kings 19, 8), as well as the forty years of Israel's wandering in the desert before reaching the promised land.

There were, however, varied ways of reckoning the forty days in different areas of the Church. The East generally spread Lent over seven weeks with both Saturdays and Sundays exempt from fasting; whereas the West had a six-week period with only Sundays exempt. Since this latter arrangement fell short of forty days, this deficiency in the Western reckoning was corrected by adding four more days, pushing the beginning of Lent to Ash Wednesday, and also adding Good Friday and Holy Saturday to the preparatory fast. It might be noted that the present arrangement of Lent (Ash Wednesday to the Mass of Holy Thursday) adds up to forty-four days if we include the six Sundays of Lent (and they are certainly very important days of Lent).

Today, of course, physical fasting and abstinence are not obligatory for the faithful on all the days of Lent as they once were. Only Ash Wednesday and Good Friday are now strict fast-and-abstinence days, while all the Fridays of Lent are abstinence days. When the forty-day period of Lent first developed there was also not that much emphasis on physical fasting as such, but a broader emphasis on the spiritual renewal demanded as preparation for the Easter celebration. Lent was a period marked by fasting, but not necessarily one in which the faithful fasted every day.

However, as time went on, more and more emphasis was placed upon fasting, and from the fifth to the ninth centuries the observance of the fast was very strict: only one meal a day toward evening was allowed, and flesh meat and fish and in most places even eggs and dairy products were also forbidden. From the ninth century on, fasting practices were relaxed somewhat: the main meal was allowed in the evening; the prohibition against fish and dairy products was also removed.

In the twentieth century more mitigations were allowed by the Holy See, permitting meat at the principal meal (except on Fridays), and there was a trend toward greater emphasis on other forms of penitential works than just fasting and abstinence. Pope Paul VI in February of 1966 issued a letter or decree (*"Poenitemini"*) which radically changed the Church regulations on fasting and abstinence, removing obligatory abstinence for Catholics on Fridays throughout the ordinary year and reducing the fast and abstinence days before Easter to Ash

Wednesday and Good Friday, together with abstinence only on all Fridays of Lent. In this decree, however, the Pope did review the general need for all "to do penance" as Christ had taught, and he recommended other types of penance which might be more suited and adapted to individuals in their lives and to the needs and conditions of modern times.

Hence, Pope Paul VI was not encouraging a lessening of penitential practices in the lives of Catholics but urging greater personal responsibility and initiative in choosing the specific ways or types of penance. This is in accord with the exhortation to Lenten penance in the *Constitution on the Liturgy* of the Second Vatican Council, in which we read: "During Lent penance should not only be internal and individual, but also external and social. The practice of penance should be fostered in ways that are possible in our own times and in different regions, and according to the circumstances of the faithful" (n. 110).

The External Characteristics of Lent

Physical fasting and abstinence and other types of bodily penance are one of the external characteristics of the Lenten season. Other more specifically liturgical external characteristics of this season are: the purple color of vestments, tabernacle, veils, antependiums, etc.; also the restricted use of flowers and organ music during this season; the omission of the Gloria and the Alleluia in the Masses of Lent; and the special Scripture texts for use at every Mass of Lent, with emphasis on Lenten themes such as penance, conversion, prayer, fasting, redemption, forgiveness, and baptism.

The Spirit or "Soul" of Lent

All the externals of Lent, however, are meant to aid and promote the goal of Lent, which is the *inner spiritual renewal* of the Church in all its members; i.e., their *growth in the life of Christ* (sanctifying grace). This we can call the "spirit" or "soul" of the season of Lent. To die with Christ in order to rise

71

and share in his life is the goal of Lent and of the whole Easter celebration. "Life," "growth," "newness" are the themes that dominate the liturgy of this season, and we need to look at these themes in greater detail and see how the externals of Lent are related to them.

1. Lent, the "Springtime" of the Church Year

The English word "Lent" comes from an old Anglo-Saxon word, "lencten," which means "spring" or "springtime." In countries of the northern hemisphere, the season of Lent parallels roughly the springtime of the natural year. Springtime in nature is the time of life, of newness, of growth! Winter was the season of dying and of inactivity, the time in nature when almost all things become lifeless and colorless; the days are cloudier, the nights longer and colder. But in spring nature comes back to life: the warm winds begin to blow, the sun rises earlier and sets later, the grass turns green again, the leaves on the trees begin to bud, the flowers to grow, the birds return from the south. Yes, spring is a time of life, newness and growth, a time of hope and joy. The forty days of Lent, whether celebrated in the northern or southern hemispheres, is the Church's "springtime" of the liturgical year. It is a time for spiritual newness or renewal, a time of growth in the divine life that Jesus has come to bring us. "I came that they may have life and have it more abundantly," Jesus had said of himself (John 10, 10). It is the reception of this life and its growth within us "more abundantly" that this spiritual springtime of Lent is all about.

This characterization of Lent as a time of renewal and growth in the life of Christ is brought out well by the first Preface of Lent that is used in Masses during Lent. Addressing God the Father, the preface says: "Each year you give us this joyful season when we prepare to celebrate the paschal mystery with mind and heart renewed. . . . As we recall the great events that gave us new life in Christ, you bring the image of your Son to perfection within us."

2. Christ, the Source of Life and Newness and Growth

It is Christ, of course, who is the source of the life and newness and growth that the springtime of Lent is meant to bring us.
The Father who has life sent Christ into the world, and Christ
has life because of this Father (John 6, 57) and we have life
through Christ and his willingness to lay down his life for us and
to take it up again (John 10, 17). It is the passion and resurrection of Christ that have brought about our redemption and have
made it possible for us to have our sins forgiven and to become
the "children of God" (1 John 3, 1), sharing in God's eternal life.
As Paul writes in the Letter to the Ephesians: "But God, who is
rich in mercy, because of the great love he had for us, even when
we were dead in our transgressions, brought us to life with
Christ (by grace you have been saved), raised us up with him,
and seated us with him in the heavens in Christ Jesus, that in the
ages to come he might show the immeasurable riches of his
grace in his kindness to us in Christ Jesus" (2, 4-7).

3. Baptism, the Sacrament of New Life

It is in the sacrament of baptism, which has always been
closely associated with the season of Lent, that Christ first
shares his life with us. The *Constitution on the Liturgy* says
that the twofold character of the season of Lent consists in "recalling or preparing for baptism" and in "penance." Baptism,
of course, is primarily the sacrament of rebirth, the sacrament
of "new life." It is the sacrament in which we first are born
again of water and the Holy Spirit and in which we put on the
Lord Jesus Christ. It is the sacrament in which we first become
united with the paschal mystery of Christ, dying with Christ and
being buried with him and then rising with him to new life. "We
indeed were buried with him through baptism into death, so
that, just as Christ was raised from the dead by the glory of the
Father, we too might live in newness of life" (Romans 6, 4).

The season of Lent is meant to prepare one for receiving
this gift of new life or to recall our baptism and all that this sac-

rament continues to mean and demand in our lives. The First Letter of Peter, within the context of a prayer of thanksgiving, gives a beautiful treatise on the deep meaning of baptism: "Blessed be the God and Father of our Lord Jesus Christ, who in his great mercy gave us new birth to a living hope through the resurrection of Jesus Christ from the dead, to an inheritance that is imperishable, undefiled, and unfading, kept in heaven for you who by the power of God are guarded through faith, to a salvation that is ready to be revealed in the final time" (1 Peter 1, 3-5).

St. Paul, on the other hand, speaks of the demands that baptism entails in the passage from the Romans quoted above: "We know that our old self was crucified with him, so that our sinful body might be done away with, that we might no longer be in slavery to sin. For a dead person has been absolved from sin. If, then, we have died with Christ, we believe that we shall also live with him. We know that Christ, raised from the dead, dies no more; death no longer has power over him. As to his death, he died to sin once and for all; as to his life, he lives for God. Consequently, you too must think of yourselves as [being] dead to sin and living for God in Christ Jesus" (Romans 6, 6-11).

The recalling of our baptism during the season of Lent, therefore, should awaken within us a deeper awareness and appreciation of what is our great calling and destiny and also inspire a firm determination to put to death sin in our lives and to be more and more alive in Christ Jesus!

The Lenten Means of Growing in the Life of Christ

To aid us in the struggle against sin and to foster the growth of Christ's life within us, the Church has for centuries offered and encouraged three practices to be observed in a special way during the forty days of Lent. These are: prayer, fasting, and almsgiving. Each of these practices is important for the spiritual renewal, the growth in Christ's life, the conversion and victory over sin that are the goal of the Lenten season.

a) Prayer

"Prayer," writes Father Nocent in his book on the liturgical year, "is the chief activity of Lent, and Lent is a time for renewal in the practice of prayer."[1] In prayer we lift our minds and hearts to God; we come near to God and allow him to draw near us. The practice of prayer — both formal and vocal prayers such as the rosary, the Mass, and the stations of the cross, and interior prayer and meditation — create the atmosphere in which the life of Christ can grow within us. Prayer is something like the warm air of spring which calls forth and nourishes the renewal of life in the world of nature. Without the spirit and practice of prayer, the life of Christ does not flourish. It is not surprising, then, that the *Constitution on the Liturgy* says that Lent is to be a "period of closer attention to the Word of God and more ardent prayer" (n. 109).

b) Fasting

The second means of growing in the life of Christ is the practice of fasting, which the Christians in earlier times considered closely related to prayer, as a source of fervor in prayer. St. Nilus, for example, expressed the relationship in this image: "The prayer of one who is fasting is like a young eagle that soars into the air, whereas the prayer of an immoderate eater is burdened by satiety and sinks earthward."

By "fasting" we usually think first of physical fasting: not eating certain foods or drink or eating less for a period of time. We can also include under this physical or external fasting such things as giving up certain forms of entertainment (movies, television, etc.) during Lent. All these types of "fasting" or penance are good and important. They help us to overcome selfishness in our lives and develop discipline and self-control in us. One of the prefaces for the Lenten Masses speaks of the rewards of such physical fasting and self-denial: "Through our observance of Lent [the older version read "through our bodily fast"] you correct our faults and raise up our minds to you, you help us grow in holiness and offer us the rewards of everlasting life through Jesus Christ our Lord."

Such bodily or external fasting is also a way of joining ourselves with the physical sufferings of Christ. Pope St. Leo spoke of this aspect of bodily fasting in these words: "The holy apostles, under the inspiration of the Holy Spirit, ordained that a greater fast should be observed during these days, in order that by a common sharing of Christ's cross, we may contribute something to what he has done for us, in accordance with the Apostle's words: 'If we have died with him, we shall also live with him!' "[2]

However, our bodily or external fasting and penances should not be viewed as an end in themselves. Rather, they must be a reminder and sign to us of the more important interior fasting and abstinence from sin. St. Augustine says on this point: "If we truly fast, we must abstain above all from sin." St. Leo speaks along these same lines: "Our fasting does not consist merely in abstinence from food; in fact, there is no profit in depriving the body of nourishment unless the spirit turns from injustice and the tongue abstains from quarreling." That same Pope and saint asked; "Of what good would it be to deprive the body of food, if one were not willing at the same time to detach the heart from sin?"[3]

c) Almsgiving or Charitable Works

The third means that the Church highly recommends and encourages us to use during Lent in our battle against sin and in our efforts to grow in the life of Christ is almsgiving or charitable works. And this practice is also seen as closely associated with the previous two practices of prayer and fasting and as the fruit of our prayer and fasting.

St. Augustine in one of his Lenten sermons stresses the importance of uniting fasting and almsgiving to our prayer as a means of allowing our prayer to truly rise up to God. He says: "By almsgiving and fasting we add wings of fervor to our prayers so that they may more easily fly up and reach God. . . . Through humility and charity, fasting and almsgiving, abstaining and forgiving, avoiding evil and doing good, our prayer seeks peace and achieves it. For such prayer takes its flight on the wings lent it by these virtues and easily reaches heaven, where Christ our Peace has gone on ahead."[4]

From the early centuries of the Church there was seen a close relationship between fasting and almsgiving, expressed in the principle: "What we forego by fasting is to be given as alms to the poor!" Or as Pope St. Leo put this principle in a more extended and striking form, "Let fasting Christians grow fat through the distribution of alms and the care of the poor. Let a person give to the weak and poor what he refuses to spend on his own pleasures."[5] Our giving up certain foods or forms of entertainment during Lent should not, therefore, be a way of saving up our money so that we can have a "blast" when Lent is over. What we save through our Lenten penances (but not only that) should be given to the poor and needy in recognition of our oneness in the family of Christ.

Our Union With Christ in Lent

In our Lenten practices of prayer and fasting and almsgiving, and in our general desire and efforts to overcome sin and to grow in the life of Christ, it is important that we unite ourselves, first of all, with Christ. This realization of Christ being united with us is a great source of fervor and perseverance in our Lenten practices. We go out into the desert for forty days not by ourselves but united with Christ and his forty-day period of fast and prayer.

Father Pius Parsch speaks of this union of ourselves with Christ during Lent in the following comments on the Gospel account of Christ's forty days in the desert, which account we read on the First Sunday of each Lenten season:

> The Gospel shows us Christ in the twofold role of one doing penance and one who is a warrior. We now follow Christ the penitent into the wilderness of renunciation in order to fast with him for forty days. Our fasting is thereby sanctified because we become united with Christ and take part in his fasting. The thought that we the members are joined with our head can make this Lenten period more sacred and important for us. The fasting of Christ is part of his whole work of salvation, and so for us, too, the forty-day period of our Lenten penance contributes to the building up of the Kingdom of God on earth. Perhaps it is the most important time of the whole year as head and members enter into the great season of penance.
>
> But the Lord also stands before us a warrior. We see in the Gospel the divine hero victorious in the threefold conflict with the devil. There stand in opposition the two princes: the prince of this world, the devil; and Christ, the prince of peace and king of the world. They engage in battle, and the prince of this world, Satan, marshals his whole army: the world with its magnificence, hell, and egoism with its insatiable desires. Christ, however, is victorious! And that battleground is still close to us — within our hearts. Our higher and lower natures battle within us. Christ must triumph in us. The thought that we are not alone in this fight should give us strength and confidence. The head and the members struggle together and triumph together![6]

Our Union with Others in Lent

A final thought that flows from the previous one is that we also carry out our Lenten penances and practices in union with all the members of the Church. God has saved us through Christ not as so many isolated individuals but as members of a family, a people that he saves. Hence, during this time of Lent, it is the entire Church on earth that is struggling against sin and Satan; it is the entire Church that is, or should be, striving to grow into the fullness of Christ's life. Every sin that we commit disfigures in some way the entire Church; every virtue that we are adorned with gives new beauty to the garment of the entire Church.

In our prayer, fasting, and almsgiving, we need to keep in mind, then, all the actual members of the Church and all the potential members; i.e., all people in the world. We need to unite ourselves with the catechumens who are preparing to receive new life in baptism at Easter, with the sinners who have strayed from Christ that they may return and receive forgiveness and renewed life, with the great majority of Christians who need to continue growing in the fullness of Christ's life, and with all who do not yet know Christ that they may be led to the fountain of living water.

Conclusion

Lent, then, is the springtime of the liturgical year — a season of newness, growth, and life. As such it should be a season of great optimism and joy, even though we do focus and meditate often on the sufferings and death of Christ. In the fullness of our faith, we must look on the sufferings and death of Christ not only in sorrow because of our sins, which caused these sufferings, but also in joy and hope because through his sufferings and death Jesus has conquered sin and death and brought us to life in him.

Hence, with optimism and joy we work with Christ in the season of Lent to create his image within us and in the whole Church and world. With Christ we strive to "pass from death to life" (Postcommunion Prayer for Friday of Fourth Week of Lent), to "pass from our old life of sin to the new life of grace" (Opening Prayer, Monday of Fifth Week of Lent). United with Christ, its head and Savior and King, the whole Church strains to attain the fullness of Christ's life, which after our sufferings and death on earth leads to the eternal life and glory of heaven!

* * * * * * *

CHAPTER SIX

'THROUGH DEATH TO LIFE'

Celebrating Holy Week

"WAS IT NOT necessary that the Messiah should suffer these things and enter into his glory?" (Luke 24, 26).

The week that we call "Holy Week" is without doubt the most important week of the liturgical year. The Church has been preparing us for this week throughout the Lenten season. Beginning with Ash Wednesday, there has been a constant crescendo in the liturgy, building up to this great and holy week.

In the first centuries of the Church, as we have mentioned earlier, there was only one feast, the Easter feast. This feast was a celebration of the paschal mysteries; that is, a celebration of the passion, burial, resurrection, and ascension of Christ. The first Christians looked at these mysteries as one event: the passover or passage of the Lord into the kingdom of God. And at first they did not feel they could separate what God had joined together.

In time, however, it became apparent that the richness of the Easter feast could be appreciated better through a more extended celebration. Thus there developed the Sacred Three Days (Triduum Sacrum) of Holy Thursday, Good Friday, and Holy Saturday - Easter Sunday. Palm Sunday was added still later as a fitting solemn beginning to this Holy Week. And, in a sense, the season of Lent and the whole of what we know today as the liturgical year was but an extension and development of the original Easter feast.

Awareness of the historical development of Holy Week from the original, one Easter feast should enable us to better appreciate an essential element of Holy Week: namely, that all of Holy Week is related to and finds its meaning in the resurrection of Christ! The crucifixion and resurrection are inseparable. Christ's work of salvation does not end with his death but includes also the triumph of his resurrection. We must see Christ's sufferings and death as the means or way to his victory and triumph manifested in his resurrection. This is the way Christ himself viewed his passion and death: "Was it not necessary that the Messiah should suffer these things and enter into his glory?" (Luke 24, 26).

Thus, through the whole of this week, there sounds, at least in the background, a triumphant, joyful note which sees in the sufferings of Christ the way to the glory of the resurrection. In each day of this week this motif will be present in some way in the liturgy (e.g., the joyful homage to Christ as King on Palm Sunday; the festive celebration of the Last Supper on Holy Thursday; the unveiling and exaltation of the cross as a sign of victory on Good Friday; the jubilant remembrance and reenactment of the Passover on Holy Saturday).

"Keep in mind that Jesus Christ has died for us and is risen from the dead. He is our saving Lord, he is joy for all ages."

Palm (Passion) Sunday

"With palms let us welcome the Lord as he comes, with songs and hymns let us run to meet him, as we offer him our joyful worship and sing: Blessed be the Lord!" (Antiphon for Canticle of Zechariah).

The Spirit of the Palm Sunday Liturgy

The liturgy of Palm or Passion Sunday (like that of Holy Thursday and Good Friday) is *a reenactment of history*. The Christian community gathers to act out a kind of drama which makes vivid the lessons of faith found so abundantly in the Gospel accounts of the last week of Jesus' life. It is one of the few times in the liturgical year that this is done. More often we simply reflect upon the great events of salvation and use signs and symbols to make their meaning vivid. But in Holy Week we actually put ourselves into the events and act them out.

It was around the year 400 when the first attempts were made to reenact in great detail the Lord's entry into Jerusalem. And what better place to reenact this event than in Jerusalem. Egeria, a woman pilgrim in Jerusalem at this time, describes the Palm Sunday procession as it was then celebrated in Jerusalem:

> As the eleventh hour [five o'clock in the afternoon] draws near, that particular passage from scripture is read in which the children bearing palms and branches came forth to meet the Lord, saying: "Blessed is he who comes in the name of the Lord." The bishop and all the people rise immediately, and then everyone walks down from the top of the Mount of Olives, with the people preceding the bishop and responding continually with "Blessed is he who comes in the name of the Lord" to the hymns and antiphons. All the children who are present here, including those who are not able to walk because they are too young and therefore are carried on their parents' shoulders, all of them bear branches,

some carrying palms, others, olive branches. And the bishop is led in the same manner as the Lord was once led. From the top of the mountain as far as the city, and from there through the entire city as far as the Anastasis, everyone accompanies the bishop the whole way on foot, and this includes distinguished ladies and men of consequence, reciting the responses all the while, and they move very slowly so that the people will not tire. By the time they arrive at the Anastasis, it is already evening. Once they have arrived there, even though it is evening, vespers is celebrated; then a prayer is said at the cross and the people are dismissed.[1]

Other dramatic touches were added to the Palm Sunday procession in later times. In Egypt, for example, the cross, representing Christ, was carried in triumph on Palm Sunday, and in Jerusalem the bishop representing Christ later rode on a donkey in the procession.

Hence, on Palm Sunday we reenact above all the triumphant entry of Christ into Jerusalem. This entry into Jerusalem is the solemn entrance of Christ into his passion, death, and resurrection, the events which will bring about his longed-for victory over sin and death and Satan. With the freedom of a king, Jesus advances toward his death. With great willingness and love he enters on the path which will lead to the sacrificial offering of laying down his life for his friends.

From one aspect we can thus designate Palm Sunday as *a feast of Christ the King*. On this day, for the first time in his public life, Jesus allowed the homage of a king to be given him as he entered Jerusalem, the "City of the Great King." His claim to be a king was the chief grounds for his condemnation to death, and so Jesus is a martyr of his title as king. The Church, therefore, prepares for Christ on this day the homage of a king, and Palm Sunday is for us a day of public profession of our faith in Christ as king. The palm branches that we carry and the procession to the church are a joyful expression of our faith and loyalty to Christ our King.

The Drama of Palm Sunday

The Palm Sunday liturgy can be considered as a holy drama or play in which all of us are not just spectators but actors in the play. We can divide this drama into three acts.

Act One: The Blessing of Palms *(Takes place in a secondary chapel or place outside the church, which place represents the Mount of Olives.)*

The cast consists of Christ (represented by the celebrant) and the crowd of disciples (our part). As the celebrant approaches we greet him as Christ with the song of the disciples: "Hosanna to the Son of David, the King of Israel. Blessed is he who comes in the name of the Lord. Hosanna to the Son of David!" The priest then greets the people and blesses the palm branches. Then the Gospel reading describing the solemn entrance of Christ into Jerusalem is proclaimed.

Act Two: The Procession with the Blessed Branches to Jerusalem

In the second act we enthusiastically accompany Christ into Jerusalem with joyful songs, acclaiming him as our King. As knights of Christ and martyrs (witnesses) ourselves, we gather around the King of Martyrs as he freely and willingly goes to meet his death. Publicly pledging our loyalty to him, we march with Christ into his city, "Jerusalem," symbolized by the parish church.

Father Nocent, in his treatise on the liturgical year, says this about the meaning of the procession with palms:

> In this procession we are to see much more than a mimetic reminder; we are to see the ascent of God's people, and our own ascent, with Jesus to the sacrifice. Moreover, although the procession recalls Christ's triumph at Jerusalem, it leads us here and now to the Sacrifice of the Cross as rendered present in the sacrifice of the Mass that is soon to be celebrated. If we were to see in

the procession only a crowd waving palms and singing joyous songs, we would miss its real significance in the Roman liturgy. That liturgy looks upon the procession not simply as a commemoration of Christ's entry into Jerusalem nor simply as a triumphal march, but as Christ's journey, together with his people, to Calvary and the great central act of redemption.[2]

Act Three: The Celebration of Mass

In Act Three we enter with Christ into the holy city. But why has Christ come here? Is it to have himself crowned as king? No, he has come to suffer. And thus suddenly the mood of the liturgy changes and our thoughts are directed to the passion and death of Christ.

The *Opening Prayer* of the celebrant introduces the theme: the Son was sent to die, to give his life on the cross for us so that we might be saved. May we follow the example of his suffering and so share in his resurrection!

In the *First Reading* from the Book of the Prophet Isaiah, Christ himself takes center stage and, through the words of the prophet, speaks about his passion. Christ tells us of his total consecration to the divine will of his Father, and of his conviction that God will sustain him through all insults and sufferings that he must bear in order to carry out that divine will.

In the *Responsorial Psalm* Christ continues to speak in the words of Psalm 21, pouring out his heart to the Father, first with the greatest feeling of loneliness and helplessness, but finally with trust and gratitude.

Then St. Paul, the great apostle and preacher of the cross, enters onstage to speak his piece in the *Second Reading*. In words from the Letter to the Philippians, Paul urges us, the audience, to have the same mind, the same attitude that Christ had. He describes with the words of an early liturgical hymn to Christ what this attitude of Christ was; namely, one of humility and obedience by which he emptied himself and became the servant of all, laying down his life for all. And, because of this humble obedience and his freely elected self-abasement, the Father has raised Christ up and crowded him with the highest honor and glory.

After Paul has finished, the *Passion of Christ* according to one of the synoptic evangelists is read. In this reading of the Passion acount in the Palm Sunday drama, we have unfolded before us not just the bare, historical events of the final hours of Jesus, but the real faith-dimensions and epoch-making character of these events. The accounts reveal that, despite appearances, this is the "hour," God's moment in human history: the death of Christ is a redemptive death, and his resurrection is a life-giving act. This is the great culminating moment of God's saving plan for the human race!

The *Prayer Over the Gifts* indicates that the perfect sacrifice of Christ's suffering and death is renewed in the Sacrifice of the Mass, and we ask that this sacrifice may make us pleasing to God and win for us again his mercy and love.

The *Communion Antiphon* ("Father, if it is not possible that this cup pass without my drinking it, your will be done!") points up the connection between our reception of the bread and wine with the sufferings of Christ. In communion we are joined with the humble, suffering, and obedient Christ. Christ gives himself to us as spiritual food and drink to enable us to follow his example of humble submission to the Father in all things. And so, united with Christ in his death and resurrection, we are given hope and a strengthened faith and perseverance that leads to eternal salvation (*Prayer after Communion*).

Our celebration has ended We have prepared a procession of triumph for Christ, our King and Conqueror. Yet we did not allow him to march alone to the battle. In the Mass we entered in with him to the holy city, and to his death. But his dying is not the end of the drama. "By his dying he has destroyed our sins; by his rising he has raised us up to holiness of life" (Preface for Palm Sunday). The drama continues. And if we remain loyal to Christ in life and its battles, so will we march in with him one day into the new and heavenly Jerusalem, there to reign with him for ever. Then only will the final curtain be drawn!

A Homily on the Palm Sunday Feast

In the *Office of Readings* of the Liturgy of the Hours for Palm Sunday we find a beautiful selection from a sermon of St. Andrew of Crete, a bishop of the Church. I would like to include it here as we close our treatment of the Palm Sunday liturgy:

> Let us go together to meet Christ on the Mount of Olives. Today he returns from Bethany and proceeds of his own free will toward his holy and blessed passion, to consummate the mystery of our salvation. He who came down from heaven to raise us from the depths of sin, to raise us with himself, we are told in Scripture, "above every sovereignty, authority, and power, and every other name that can be named," now comes of his own free will to make his journey to Jerusalem. He comes without pomp or ostentation. As the psalmist says: "He will not dispute or raise his voice to make it heard in the streets." He will be meek and humble, and he will make his entry in simplicity.
>
> Let us accompany him as he hastens toward his passion, and imitate those who met him then, not by covering his path with garments, olive branches or palms, but by doing all we can to prostrate ourselves before him by being humble and by trying to live as he would wish. Then we shall be able to receive the Word at his coming, and God, whom no limits can contain, will be within us.
>
> In his humility Christ entered the dark regions of our fallen world and he is glad that he became so humble for our sake, glad that he came and lived among us and shared in our nature in order to raise us up again to himself. And even though we are told that he has now ascended above the highest heavens — the proof, surely, of his power and godhead — his love for man will never rest until he has raised our earthbound nature from glory to glory, and make it one with his own in heaven.
>
> So let us spread before his feet, not garments or soulless olive

branches, which delight the eye for a few hours and wither, but ourselves, clothed in his grace, or rather, clothed completely in him. We who have been baptized into Christ must ourselves be the garments that we spread before him. Now that the crimson stains of our sins have been washed away in the saving waters of baptism and we have become white as pure wool, let us present the conqueror of death, not with mere branches of palms but with the real rewards of his victory. Let our souls take the place of the welcoming branches as we join today in the children's holy song: "Blessed is he who comes in the name of the Lord. Blessed is the king of Israel."

Monday, Tuesday, and Wednesday of Holy Week

Monday, Tuesday, and Wednesday of Holy Week are lesser days, liturgically speaking, than Palm Sunday and the final three days of Holy Week. These days do, however, advance the consideration of the historical events of Christ's passion by presenting certain scenes from this passion and keeping before our eyes the great mystery of Christ's passage through death to life.

We present here just a few comments on the Scripture readings for the Masses of these three days of Holy Week.

Monday of Holy Week

The *First Reading* of each of these three days is from the Songs of the Servant of Yahweh found in the Book of the Prophet Isaiah. The reading on Monday is from the first of these Songs of the Servant and tells how this Servant has been chosen to bring hope and salvation to all nations. In his own person he will be a new covenant and a light to the world. The *Responsorial Verse* ("The Lord is my light and my salvation") echoes this theme of the First Reading.

The Gospel selection (John 12, 1-11) describes the memorable banquet in the house of Lazarus. Mary anoints Jesus' feet for his "burial" and wipes them with her hair. Judas, in contrast, resents this action of Mary and resolves to betray his master. Thus, this occasion becomes a funeral banquet that brought death (Judas) and prepared for Christ's burial (Mary).

Tuesday of Holy Week

The Second Song of the Servant of Yahweh is presented in the *First Reading* of today's liturgy of the word (Isaiah 49, 1-6). In this song the Servant himself speaks to all people. He announces that God has chosen him from his mother's womb for a special task and has been with him in all his trials. That special task is to lead Israel back to God and to bring salvation to all nations.

In the *Gospel* passage today (John 13, 21-33; 36-38) we find Jesus "troubled in spirit" at the onset of the final conflict. Christ foretells that Judas is about to betray him and that Peter, too, will disown him. Yet Jesus also speaks of being "glorified" soon by his death.

Wednesday of Holy Week

The Third Song of the Servants of Yahweh serves as our *First Reading* on Wednesday (Isaiah 50, 4-9). The Servant again speaks to us, and his song today is an act of confidence and trust in God. He describes his openness to God, receiving from him the word he is to preach to others. Yet in carrying out his mission he was persecuted, but accepted this suffering as part of his mission. And he is so certain that God is with him that he openly challenges his oppressors to appear before God with him. This same spirit of trust in God, despite suffering and rejection, is found in the *Responsorial Psalm*: "For the Lord hears the poor, and his own who are in bonds he spurns not."

The *Gospel* selection today skillfully sets the stage for the solemn commemoration of the passion, death and resurrection of Christ on Holy Thursday, Good Friday, and Holy Saturday -

Easter Sunday. "My appointed time draws near," Jesus says. Preparations are made for the celebration of Passover for Jesus with his disciples, and Judas has concluded his pact with the chief priests and is looking for an opportunity to hand Jesus over.

St. Augustine, in the Second Reading of the Liturgy of the Hours for this day, adds this reflection on the impending death of Christ: "Jesus had the power of laying down his life; we by contrast cannot choose the length of our lives, and we die even if it is against our will. He, by dying, destroyed death in himself; we are freed from death only in his death. His body did not see corruption; our body will see corruption and only then be clothed through him in incorruption at the end of the world. He needed no help from us in saving us; without him we can do nothing. He gave himself to us as the vine of the branches; apart from him we cannot have life."

Thursday of the Lord's Supper

The ancient name for this feast is "Thursday of the Lord's Supper." The title indicates the chief event or focus of this feast; namely, the institution of the Eucharistic Sacrifice at the Last Supper which the Lord shared with his apostles. As the *Constitution on the Sacred Liturgy* so well states:

At the Last Supper, on the night when he was betrayed, our Savior instituted the eucharistic sacrifice of his Body and Blood. He did this in order to perpetuate the sacrifice of the Cross throughout the centuries until he should come again, and so to entrust to his beloved spouse, the Church, a memorial of his death and resurrection: a sacrament of love, a sign of unity, a bond of charity, a paschal banquet in which Christ is consumed, the mind is filled with grace, and a pledge of future glory is given to us (n. 47).

Events Surrounding the Last Supper

It might be useful here to trace briefly the events surrounding the Last Supper as we find them related in the Gospels: In the afternoon Jesus sent his two beloved disciples Peter and John from Bethany into the city of Jerusalem to prepare the Passover lamb and the other things needed for the Passover meal. In the late afternoon Jesus himself left Bethany and traveled over the Mount of Olives to the Last Supper room. After the sun had set, the meal began.

There was first the eating of the Passover lamb; next the washing of the feet; then the unmasking of the betrayer; then the institution of the Holy Eucharist, followed in John's Gospel by the Last Discourse and High-Priestly Prayer of Jesus. After this Jesus left with his disciples to go to the Garden of Gethsemane, where he suffered his agony and where he was arrested and then taken to the Sanhedrin for interrogation and condemnation.

The Mass of the Lord's Supper

Our Mass or Eucharistic Celebration on this evening of Holy Thursday has a very special significance. It is the reenactment of the Last Supper, the first Holy Mass. The tabernacle is empty; all new hosts are freshly consecrated; we are gathered in spirit with the apostles and Christians throughout the world to receive from Jesus the gift of his own flesh and blood as if for the first time. Jesus gives us the sacred meal that will unite throughout the ages the members of his Church to himself. Today is, therefore, the "Day of Christian Community," the day of union of all Christians with one another in Christ. And because we all belong to this one community in Christ, we must also love and serve one another as Christ has loved and served us.

1. Introductory Rites

Our celebration begins on a joyful note. The altar is decorated; the priests enter clothed in festive white vestments; the

Entrance Antiphon has a triumphal ring; the "Gloria" is sung accompanied by the ringing of bells. The beautiful *Opening Prayer* spells out for us the purpose of our gathering and the results that we hope for from our celebration: we are gathered to share in the supper that Jesus gave us as a sign of his love, and we pray that we might find the fullness of this love and life.

2. The Liturgy of the Word: A Lesson on the Meaning of the Eucharist

In the Liturgy of the Word we are instructed about the meaning of the Eucharistic Sacrifice. The *First Reading* from the Book of Exodus describes the Passover rite which was celebrated every year by the Jews as a memorial of what God had done in Egypt to deliver his people from slavery. The Jews recalled in this rite that they had been saved by the blood of the lamb and that they had been led through the waters of the Red Sea to freedom. Christ is the new Passover lamb who was slain to save his people and who gives us himself as food in the new Passover rite of the Mass. Each Mass is a memorial in which we recall the great saving deeds of Christ in our lives: the shedding of his blood on the cross and his resurrection, by which we, the new people of God, have been led from the slavery of sin through the waters of baptism to the promised land of heaven.

A homily of Bishop St. Melito of Sardis, found in the Liturgy of the Hours for this day, eloquently compares Christ with the Passover lamb: "He was led forth like a lamb; he was slaughtered like a sheep. He ransomed us from our servitude to the world, as he had ransomed Israel from the land of Egypt; he freed us from the slavery of the devil, as he had freed Israel from the hand of Pharaoh. He sealed our souls with his own Spirit, and the members of our body with his own blood. . . ."

The *Responsorial Song* expands on the theme of the blood of Christ, the New Testament lamb. In the "blessing cup" (the Eucharist) we are united with the saving deeds of Christ and with one another. And in the Eucharistic Sacrifice we also make a return sacrifice of thanksgiving for all the good the Lord has done for us (Psalm 116).

In the *Second Reading* from 1 Corinthians, the Apostle Paul instructs us further on the meaning of the Eucharist. In the Eucharist, Paul tells us, we celebrate *what Christ did for us*: the Eucharist shows forth and presents anew the saving death of Christ. It is the sign of his abiding presence with his Church, reminding us of Calvary and pointing forward to the time when Christ will come again.

As we greet the Lord in the *Verse before the Gospel*, we hear his special "command" (Latin, *"mandatum"*; Old English, "maundy," whence the name "Maundy Thursday"). We are to love one another as he has loved us.

Then in the *Gospel passage* we are presented with a concrete example of Christ's humble, loving service. Christ's washing of his disciples' feet symbolizes first of all Jesus' saving death. This death will be an act of lowliness and service, entirely cleansing all the disciples except the betrayer and giving them a share in Jesus' heritage. The washing of the feet also is an example which the apostles and all of us are to follow in our lives. It is the way we live out the Mass. We are not to lord it over one another, but to serve one another in a spirit of lowliness. Hence, we can have no share in Christ's heritage, no true union with him in the Eucharist unless we are prepared to follow his example of loving service.

3. The Washing of the Feet Ceremony

After the Gospel and Homily on this feast there follows the ceremony of the washing of feet, in which the celebrant, as a representative of Christ, washes the feet of twelve people who symbolize the twelve apostles. The rite is meant, of course, to remind us graphically of the "command" of the Lord: "If I, your Lord and Master, have washed your feet, then surely you must wash one another's feet. . . . Love one another as I have loved you" (Antiphons 3 and 4 of the Washing of the Feet Rite).

4. The Liturgy of the Eucharist

As we proceed in the Evening Mass of the Lord's Supper, we reenact further what the Lord did on that evening before his death. The earlier themes of the Scripture Readings are re-echoed in the other prayers of the Mass for this night: the Sacrifice of the Mass is a reenactment of our redemption (*Prayer Over the Gifts*); Christ's gift of his body and his blood seals the new covenant (*Communion Antiphon*); Jesus "is the true and eternal priest / who established this unending sacrifice. / He offered himself as a victim for our deliverance / and taught us to make this offering in his memory. / As we eat his body which he gave for us, / we grow in strength. / As we drink his blood poured out for us, / we are washed clean" (*Preface*); the Eucharistic meal is a foreshadowing and partaking of the eternal banquet of heaven (*Prayer after Communion*).

5. Transfer of the Holy Eucharist and Watching with Christ

After the celebration of the Lord's Supper we follow the Lord to the Altar of Repose as we sing the famous "*Pange 'Lingua*" hymn, which commemorates Christ's institution of the Holy Eucharist.

There at the Altar of Repose in the hours following the Mass, we commemorate Christ's agony in the garden, as we "watch and pray" with Christ.

Friday of the Lord's Passion

The official name given to the liturgy of Good Friday is "The Celebration of Our Lord's Passion." In our country we usually refer to this day as "Good Friday" (probably a corruption of "God's Friday"), which now seems appropriate because Christ was so good to us by offering up his life for us on the cross. The central theme of the day is, then, the unselfish love and goodness of Christ shown to us most clearly by his passion and death on the cross. The shadow of that cross has fallen across every liturgy during Holy Week. Today the cross is the symbol that dominates the liturgical service.

Good Friday, however, is not a day of great sadness, but a day of prayerful consideration of the suffering and crucified Savior, who by his sufferings and death on the cross has saved us from eternal death. Indeed, a joyful strain is evident in many parts of the liturgy for Good Friday. We look upon the cross not only as the terrible instrument on which our Savior suffered and died, but also as the glorious cross or tree which our Lord willingly mounted and on which he triumphed over sin and darkness.

The liturgical service for this day is divided into three parts: the Liturgy of the Word, the Veneration of the Cross, and the Reception of Holy Communion.

The Liturgy of the Word

1. Entrance Rite

The service begins today in silence. The celebrant, dressed in red vestments, enters the chapel and goes to the altar. He bows to the altar and then prostrates himself (or kneels) in the sanctuary as a sign of mankind's helplessness and sinfulness before the all-holy God. Only through Christ's coming into the world and his death and resurrection have we been able to overcome this sinfulness and helplessness.

In the *Opening Prayer* we pray that we who have been like the sinful Adam may become like Christ, who has saved us from death by his sufferings.

2. Scripture Reading

The *First Reading* is the beautiful and moving "Fourth Song of the Servant of Yahweh" from the Book of Isaiah. The reading gives us a vivid description of the sufferings of Jesus and the reason for these sufferings: Jesus was "pierced for our offenses, crushed for our sins." But already the first line of the reading indicates that the Servant (Jesus) will be raised up and greatly exalted before the world after his suffering.

We respond to this first reading by joining ourselves with Christ and entrusting ourselves into the Father's hands: "Father, I put my life in your hands" (*Responsorial Psalm*).

The Letter to the Hebrews provides our *Second Reading* in this liturgy. And what consoling good news this passage proclaims: Jesus is our High Priest who has undergone every suffering and temptation that we experience so that he can sympathize with us and understand our weakness; as our High Priest, Jesus has prayed for us, and his prayer has been heard; and, because of his obedience and suffering, this High Priest has become "the source of eternal salvation to all who obey him."

We listen next to *St. John's Account of the Passion* of Christ. In contrast to the other Gospel writers, who stress the human side of Christ in their accounts, John shows us the suffering Savior as God and King. John stresses the divine nature of Christ and the freedom with which Jesus laid down his life for us. We see Jesus as the King ruling from the throne of the cross. "And when I am lifted up from the earth, I will draw everyone to myself" (John 12, 32).

3. The General Intercessions

The General Intercessions conclude the Liturgy of the Word for the Good Friday service. On this day the liturgy provides a series of solemn petitions for all classes and needs of the Church and of all the world. Christ died for all people, and in these solemn prayers we interpret, as it were, the mind and heart of Christ as he was lifted up and drawing all to himself.

The Unveiling and Veneration of the Cross

The second main part of the Good Friday liturgy is the unveiling and veneration of the cross, which is the sign of our redemption. This rite is very ancient and originated in Jerusalem, where the authentic wood of the cross was honored and kissed.

1. The Showing of the Cross

In our present revised liturgy there are two forms of showing the cross: one, a three-step unveiling; the other, a three-step showing of the already uncovered cross. In both forms the liturgy is focusing our attention on the cross and its victim, as the priest proclaims: "This is the wood of the cross, on which hung the Savior of the world."

2. The Veneration of the Cross

Next the priest and ministers and people approach the cross in a kind of procession, offering an appropriate sign of reverence according to local custom. (Kissing the feet of the cross is probably the most common and most fitting sign in our country.) This kiss or other act of homage should be for us one of the high points of our participation in the service. This kiss should be a sign of *sorrow* for the sins that have made the passion and death of Christ necessary; the kiss should also be a sign of our *sympathy* for Christ in his sufferings; finally, it should express our sincere *love* for Christ and the complete *dedication* of our lives to him who died for us!

3. Songs during the Veneration

During the veneration of the cross, there is sung the very moving song called the *Improperia* or *Reproaches*. This song is cast in the form of a series of complaints of Christ against his unfaithful people for their ingratitude and sinful rebellion. The accusations recall the great deeds that God worked for his people in the Old Testament times and masterfully contrast these deeds with the ungrateful response of his people. Though the accusations refer to the people of Israel in their original setting, they are meant for all persons who have shown similar ingratitude to Christ in spite of all he has done for us. Repeatedly we hear the refrain that includes us: "My people, what have I done to you? How have I offended you? Answer me!"

Another ancient response or song that may be sung during

the veneration of the cross is one that gives praise to Christ as God: "Holy is God! Holy and strong! Holy Immortal One, have mercy on us!" This refrain, sung before the now unveiled cross, is a splendid confession of faith in the crucified Christ as the Son of God.

A third antiphon that may be sung at the time of veneration is a song of joy over the cross and resurrection of Christ: "We worship you, Lord, we venerate your cross, we praise your resurrection. Through the cross you brought joy to the world."

The Holy Communion Service

The final part of the Celebration of the Lord's Passion is the reception of Holy Communion. This is a fitting conclusion to our Good Friday liturgy. We have been trying to enter as fully as possible into the passion and death of Jesus. First, we were united to Christ with our minds as we listened to the readings about his sufferings and death. Then we were united with Christ our High Priest in prayer as we begged for the needs of the Church and the world. Next we were united with Christ in our hearts and emotions as we venerated the cross and joined ourselves to Jesus in sorrow, sympathy, love, and dedication through our homage of the cross. Now, in the Holy Eucharist, we join ourselves sacramentally to Christ. This is the most perfect union we can have here on earth with Christ's passion and death: receiving into our bodies and hearts the paschal Lamb who was slain for us and who hung on the cross for our salvation. And, in this reception of the crucified Christ, we are united also with his triumph over death and sin. Thus, our sharing in the Lord's passion and death leads us to share in the new life of his resurrection! "If, then, we have died with Christ, we believe we shall also live with him" (Romans 6, 8).

Holy Saturday

"Something strange is happening — there is a great silence

on earth today, a great silence and stillness. The whole earth keeps silence because the King is asleep. The earth trembled and is still because God has fallen asleep in the flesh and he has raised up all who have slept ever since the world began. God has died in the flesh and hell trembles with fear" (Second Reading of the Liturgy of the Hours).

These words from an ancient homily on Holy Saturday characterize the mood or spirit of the Church from the waning hours of Good Friday throughout the hours of Saturday until the Easter Vigil begins. It is a sacred day of rest, a time of transition from the Lenten observance of prayer and penance into an anticipation of joy in the resurrection.

Except for the Liturgy of the Hours, whose prayer for this day is characterized by the spirit of peace, rest, and quiet consideration of the Lord in the tomb, there is no liturgical ceremony on this day until after nightfall. This void is intended to heighten the Christian's expectation of the resurrection event: the Church keeps watch at the tomb of Christ.

The Easter Vigil

"The Great Night," "Night of Nights," "The Mother of All Vigils," "The Solemnity of Solemnities," "The Feast of Feasts," "the culminating point of the Christian liturgy" — these are but some of the titles and descriptions given to the Easter Vigil Service, suggesting its importance and preeminence in the liturgical life of the Church.

It is easy to cite such encomiums. But just what makes this Easter Vigil so outstanding and so important? Why is it "the Great Night," "The Feast of Feasts," "the culminating point of the Christian liturgy"?

The basic answer to these questions is, I believe, that the Easter Vigil Service is so important and preeminent because it is the most solemn celebration in the entire year of the central mystery of our redemption: the saving death and resurrection of

Jesus Christ! In every Mass at any time of the year, the Church does, of course, celebrate the mystery of Christ's death and resurrection; but in the Easter Vigil she commemorates and celebrates this death and resurrection at the most solemn time and in the most solemn manner.

1. The Most Solemn Time

The Easter Vigil Service is the most solemn celebration of the passover mystery of Christ's death and resurrection first of all because it is celebrated at the most solemn and appropriate time: namely, at night and on the very night "which alone deserved to know the time and hour in which Christ arose from the tomb" (*Exsultet*).

The Church in her liturgy generally understands how important are time and place in the symbolism of liturgical action. Thus she wisely assigns the most solemn celebration of the death and resurrection of Christ to the most appropriate time: to the night that Christ arose from the dead. It was in the darkness of night that the paschal Lamb was born again from the womb of the grave, when he conquered the darkness of sin and received the seal of divine approval in his resurrection. We do not know, to be sure, the precise hour of the resurrection, but we know that it occurred during the night that followed the paschal Sabbath. For "it was still dark" (John 20, 1) when Mary Magdalene, on the first day of the week, went to the sepulchre and found it open and empty.

2. The Most Solemn Manner

The Easter Vigil Service is also celebrated in the most solemn manner — by a "vigil" or "nightwatch" for the Lord. The present Roman Sacramentary speaks on this point as it introduces this service. "In accord with ancient tradition, this night is one of vigil for the Lord (Exodus 12, 42). The Gospel of Luke (12, 35ff) is a reminder to the faithful to have their lamps burning ready, to be like people awaiting their master's return so that when he arrives he will find them wide awake and will seat them at his table."

This "night vigil for the Lord" has deep significance for our understanding and appreciation for this service and its importance, so we will study this concept in greater detail.

The Night Watch for the Lord

1. The Vigil of the Jewish Passover Observance

The idea of keeping a vigil on this night and of celebrating the Christian paschal feast during the night was a practice that the Christians took over from the Jews along with the Passover feast itself. The Christian Easter is the Jewish Passover feast given a Christian direction.

Now an important part of the Jewish Passover observance was the vigil or night watch. This vigil was seen as commemorating the vigil that God himself kept all through the night of the exodus from Egypt in order to free his people from the hands of their oppressors. The night of the Passover was kept holy therefore each year by a vigil of prayer and praise in gratitude for Yahweh's own vigil. "This was a night of vigil for the LORD, as he led them out of the land of Egypt; so on this same night all the Israelites must keep a vigil for the LORD throughout their generations" (Exodus 12, 42).

Hence, through this feast celebrated during the night, the people of Israel kept alive the memory of all that God had done for them, not only the deliverance from Egypt but all that this deliverance led to, particularly their birth as a holy nation and as the people of God. It was on this night that Israel celebrated their coming to be!

Further, the Israelites who kept the vigil each year on this night were not only recalling and commemorating the Exodus of the past, but were also holding themselves in readiness for a greater exodus and a mightier deliverance that was to come. Great as the past had been when the Lord passed among them and delivered them with an outstretched hand, this was only the pledge and the rough draft of what the future would be when God would come once again to deliver them completely and establish them forever in his kingdom. That would be the true paschal festival, not a mere commemoration, but the true and final passover.

2. The Christian Passover Vigil

When the first Christians took over the feast of the Jewish Passover and made it their Easter feast, they also commemorated, like the Jews, all that God had done for them in delivering them from sin and Satan and death and in making them the new "people of God." The Christians, like the Jews before them, also looked forward in hope and awaited the far greater deliverance that was yet to come: the return of the Lord in glory and the beginning of the perfect and eternal Easter festival of heaven.

Let us spell out some of the aspects of the Christian Easter Vigil.

a) A Vigil of Commemoration

Like the Israelites, we Christians on this night recall in faith and gratitude all that God has done for us. Especially do we recall with all possible solemnity the resurrection of our Lord, which is viewed by the liturgy not simply as the commemoration of the single act of Christ's rising from the dead, but as the completion of the whole work of his redemption of the world.

b) A Vigil of Expectation

Our Easter Vigil, however, is more than a vigil of commemoration. It is also a vigil of waiting and expectation, as mentioned above. And what is it that we expect or wait and long for in this vigil?

I like the way St. Augustine answers that question in one of his sermons on the occasion of an Easter Vigil: "We now need not wait for the Lord to arise, for Christ's resurrection was centuries ago. Nor is our annual celebration simply a commemoration of a past event; it implies a present action on our part, which we accomplish by our life of faith and of which this vigil is the symbol. The entire course of time is in fact one long night during which the Church keeps watch, waiting for the return of the Lord, waiting 'until he comes again.' "

Hence, on this one night of the year, we are doing visibly and publicly what we should be doing spiritually at all times: i.e., we are waiting and watching and hoping for the return of the Lord in glory when the work of redemption will be fully and perfectly realized. This is what the Lord urges us to do in the passage from Luke referred to in the Sacramentary introduction to the vigil service: "Let your belts be fastened around your waists and your lamps be burning ready. Be like people awaiting their master's return from a wedding, so that when he arrives and knocks, you will open for him without delay. It will go well with those servants when the master finds them wide-awake on his return. I tell you, he will put on an apron, seat them at table, and proceed to wait on them."

This aspect of expectation in the Easter Vigil was so prominent in the early Church that some of the Fathers believed that the Lord will come in final judgment at midnight of the holy night of Easter. Lactantius, writing in A.D. 310, says: "This night is twice holy; for it was in this night that the Lord after his passion returned to life; and it is on this same night that he will come to take possession of his empire over all the universe."

c) A Vigil of Initiation and Rejuvenation

Finally, the Easter Vigil is a vigil of initiation and rejuvenation in which we meet the Lord here and now in the present in the sacraments of initiation and rejuvenation: baptism, confirmation, and the Eucharist. With a vigil of commemoration we recall the *past* saving deeds of God that culminate in the resurrection of Christ. As a vigil of expectation we look forward to the future and the return of Christ in glory. But with a vigil of initiation and rejuvenation we are united with Christ in the sacraments in the *present* and share the bounty of his risen life.

In this vigil of initiation, the candidates for baptism are admitted to the rebirth of water and the Spirit which will incorporate them visibly into the visible Church and mystically into Christ. On this night the seed of the resurrection is implanted into them, for in baptism they are buried together with Christ and raised up with him to live a new life. Also on this night, the newly baptized (if adults) may receive the sacrament of confirmation and assist at the Holy Eucharist, receiving the body and blood of Christ for the first time in Holy Communion. These three sacraments of baptism, confirmation and the Holy Eucharist are the sacraments of Christian initiation.

But this liturgy of initiation is not just for the new members of the Church. It is meant for all the members of God's people. For all the faithful it is the common anniversary of baptism, our initiation into the Church. Hence, in the vigil service we renew our profession of faith in the crucified and risen Lord and renew our solemn promise to serve God faithfully and be loyal to Christ (*Renewal of Baptismal Promises*).

Moreover, the liturgy of initiation brings to all the grace of renewal or spiritual rejuvenation. The Easter Vigil rites increase our consciousness of incorporation into Christ, our assimilation to him in his mystery of suffering and glory, of death and life. By word and sacrament we are united again in the Easter Vigil liturgy with the risen Lord and we grow in his life and grace. "This is the night when Christians everywhere, washed clean of sin and freed from all defilement, are restored to grace and grow together."

The Parts of the Easter Vigil Service

"The night vigil is arranged in four parts: a brief Service of Light; the Liturgy of the Word, in which the Church meditates on the wonderful things God has done for his people from the beginning; the Liturgy of Baptism, when new members of the Church are reborn as the day of resurrection approaches; and the Liturgy of the Eucharist, when the whole Church is called to the table which the Lord has prepared for his people through his death and resurrection" (*The Roman Sacramentary*).

These ceremonies of the Easter Vigil are so rich in their historical background and significance that we cannot present a thorough treatment of every ceremony, but we will concentrate on the principal aspects and symbolism of these rites.

1. Solemn Beginning: The Service of Light

The opening ceremony of the Easter Vigil is the Service of Light. It is a ceremony rich in word and symbol and centers around the paschal candle, which is the great symbol of the risen Lord, "the light of the world." On Easter night, Christ arose shining and resplendent as the sun, thereby conquering forever the dark night of sin.

a) The Blessing of the New Fire

The blessing of the new fire is a rite that is subordinate to the blessing of the Paschal Candle and the procession. The prayer for the blessing of the fire reminds us that we share in the light of the Father's glory through Christ, who is the light of the world. And we pray that God might also set us on fire with hope and purify our minds by the Easter celebration so that one day we might celebrate the feast of eternal light in heaven.

b) The Lighting of the Easter Candle

The paschal candle is lighted from the new fire by the celebrant as he proclaims: "May the light of Christ, rising in glory, dispel the darkness of our hearts and minds!" Behold the symbol of the glory and splendor of Christ's risen presence among us! Through his rising he has made it possible for us to overcome the darkness of sin and death. "I am the light of the world.

Whoever follows me will not walk in darkness, but will have the light of life" (John 8, 12).

c) The Procession with the Easter Candle

The full meaning of the paschal candle is seen when this newly blessed "pillar of fire," carried by a deacon or the celebrant, leads the way into the darkened church. As it goes foreward it sheds its beams and scatters the darkness before it. As God led the Israelites by a pillar of fire out of the slavery of Egypt and on through the desert to the promised land, so does the risen Christ lead us from the bondage of sin through the journey of life to the promised land of heaven. And Christ shares with his followers his "light of life" (the lighting of the candles of all in the procession) and expects us also to assist him in spreading this light to all (our passing on the light to others around us).

"Christ our light!" the deacon proclaims three times, and all answer, "Thanks be to God!" Thanks be to God for the resurrection of Christ and for our own share in this resurrection! Thanks be to God for his wonderful care and merciful and boundless love! Thanks be to God, who has given us so great a Redeemer! Thanks be to God, who has delivered us out of darkness and brought us into his marvelous light!

d) The Easter Proclamation

The above response of praise and thanks to God is taken up in a solemn and jubilant way in the Easter proclamation, which follows the procession and brings to a close the Service of Light. As all stand with their own lighted candles facing the Easter candle, the deacon or another cantor proclaims the glorious hymn which is known as the "*Exsultet*" from that first word in the original Latin text.

This "*Exsultet*" is a hymn that speaks of a threefold Easter or Passover night: the Old Testament Passover; the Passover of Jesus from death to resurrection; and the sacramental representation of the Passover in the Easter Vigil itself, by which we share in Christ's resurrection.

+ The first Easter night is the prototype. It is the night on which Moses led the people out of Egypt. Of this night the Exsultet narrates the following: "This is the night when first you saved our fathers; you freed the people of Israel from their slavery and led them dry-shod through the sea. This is the night when the pillar of fire destroyed the darkness of sin."

+ The death and resurrection of Jesus are the fulfillment and perfection of this Old Testament Passover. In this new Easter Passover, "Christ, the true Lamb, is slain, whose blood consecrates the houses of all believers." Our hymn speaks eloquently and emotionally of this second Easter night: "This is the night when Jesus Christ broke the chains of death and rose triumphant from the grave. . . . Most blessed of all nights, chosen by God to see Christ rising from the dead! Of this night scripture says: 'The night will be as clear as day; it will become my light, my joy!' "

+ The third Easter night of which the *Exsultet* sings is the present Easter night in which the death and resurrection of Christ are sacramentally made present in our liturgical celebration. Christ enters into our souls and shares with us his risen life. Of this present, sacramental Easter night we hear: "This is the night when Christians everywhere, washed clean of sin and freed from all defilement, are restored to grace and grow together in holiness. . . . The power of this holy night dispels all evil, washes away guilt, restores lost innocence, brings mourners joy; it casts out hatred, brings us peace, and humbles earthly pride. Night truly blessed when heaven is wedded to earth and man is reconciled with God!"

2. The Liturgy of the Word
The instructions in the Sacramentary for the Easter Vigil

state that "the reading of the word of God is the fundamental element of the Easter Vigil." In this Liturgy of the Word for the Easter Vigil we meditate on all the wonderful things that God has done for his people from the beginning. God speaks to us in the Scripture readings and we speak to God in the responsorial psalms and in the concluding prayers. These latter often bring out beautifully the meaning or Christian significance of the readings for us today.

Reading One: **The Creation Narrative (Genesis 1, 1-2, 2)**

The first reading describes the first great and wonderful act that God has done for his people: "he created all things in wonderful beauty and order" (Oration), and made human beings in his own image and likeness to rule over all creation. An even more wonderful act of God, however, is the "new creation" by which in the fullness of time God redeemed his people through the death and resurrection of Jesus Christ.

Reading Two: **The Abraham Story (Genesis 22, 1-18)**

The second reading from the Old Testament tells of another wonderful act of God: the choosing of Abraham to be the father of a great nation in whose descendants "all the nations of the earth shall find blessing" because of Abraham's unselfish obedience to God. It is through the obedient death of Christ and his resurrection that God fulfills the promise to Abraham and establishes the new people of God.

Reading Three: **The Passage Through the Red Sea (Exodus 14, 15 - 15, 1)**

The third reading from the Book of Exodus (the only reading that must be used during the Liturgy of the Word) tells of another great and wonderful deed of God in the past: the saving of God's people of Israel from the slavery of the Egyptians and bringing them to the mountain of God's inheritance. "The Red Sea," Oration B declares, "is a symbol of our baptism." And the

Israelite nation that God has freed from slavery is "a sign of the Christian people." The Father continues to work his miraculous wonders in our day through baptism, by which he offers salvation to all mankind (Oration A).

Reading Four: **The Enduring Love of God for His People (Isaiah 54, 5-14)**

In the fourth reading from the Prophet Isaiah, we hear God speak about his enduring and tender love for us, his people, God, who is the Creator and Maker of all, is like a husband in his great love for us, his chosen people and his spouse. His love for us is so intense and personal that he takes us back again and again — us, who are like a repeatedly unfaithful wife. His love is everlasting: "Though the mountains leave their place and hills be shaken, my love shall never leave you." It is hard to find in the Old Testament books a clearer expression of God's love for his people than this one.

Reading Five: **Invitation to Come to the Lord (Isaiah 55, 1-11)**

Another passage from Isaiah serves as the fifth reading offered by the Liturgy of the Word. This passage is primarily an invitation or summons for all who are thirsty and hungry and poor to come to the Lord who alone can slake our real hungers and thirsts and make us truly rich by sharing his life with us. God has promised and his word will achieve its end. In the sacraments, particularly in baptism and the Holy Eucharist, do we come to the Lord and "draw water joyfully from the springs of salvation" (Responsorial Song).

Reading Six: **Walk in the Way of the Lord (Baruch 3, 9-15, 32-34)**

A passage from the Prophet Baruch provides our sixth reading on this night. The reading is an exhortation not to abandon the fountain of wisdom but to walk in the way of the Lord — to walk by the light of the wisdom of God, walk by that light toward splendor.

Where do we find the fountain of wisdom? How do we walk in the way of the Lord? Jesus has told us: "I am the way and the truth and the life; no one comes to the Father except through me" (John 14, 6). "Do you also want to forsake me, the fountain of wisdom?" Jesus asks us this night. Let us respond with Peter in great faith and love: "Lord, to whom shall we go? You have the words of eternal life" (Responsorial Verse).

Reading Seven: Promise of Regeneration (Ezechiel 36, 16-17; 18-28)

Our seventh and final reading from the Old Testament for the Vigil Service is from the Book of the Prophet Ezekiel. God, through his prophet, speaks to us again in this selection and promises to bring about a regeneration, a restoring to life after Israel had sinned and turned away from God. We hear that God will sprinkle clean water upon his people and give them a new heart and spirit. God has fulfilled this promise of regeneration through the resurrection of Christ, in which regeneration we participate through baptism and the other sacraments.

The Gloria and Opening Prayer

At this point in the Liturgy of the Word the reading from Scripture are interrupted by the singing of the joyful "Glory to God in the highest." This is followed by an oration which embodies some of the main themes of the Vigil Service: the radiance of the risen Christ brightens the night and he recreates and renews us in mind and body so that we might give ourselves more completely to the service of God.

The Epistle Reading: Our Share in Christ's Death and Resurrection (Romans 6, 3-11)

The Epistle readings of the Vigil from the Letter to the Romans speaks of the great mystery and meaning of baptism.

Through baptism we share in the paschal mystery, the death and rising of Jesus. Our old sinful self is crucified with Christ and we are thereby freed from the slavery of sin. We rise with Christ and share the new life that Christ now enjoys. The early form of baptism by submersion in a pool of water symbolized most strikingly this dying and being buried and then rising to new life with him. Having risen with Christ, Paul goes on to admonish us that we must now walk in this new life, considering ourselves "dead to sin but alive for God in Christ Jesus."

The Easter Alleluia

We reach in the singing of the threefold "Alleluia" before the Gospel another highpoint of the Liturgy of the Word. The "Alleluia," the Easter song par excellence, has not been heard in the liturgy since the beginning of Lent. It is now intoned by the celebrant or a cantor as an expression of the meaning and joy of Easter. "We are Easter people and Alleluia is our song" (St. Augustine).

The Gospel Reading: **He Has Been Raised Up! (Matthew 28, 1-10; Mark 16, 1-8; Luke 24, 1-12)**

In all the three-cycle Gospel readings for this night we find the announcement of the good news of Christ's resurrection made by an angel: "He has been raised; he is not here" (Mark); "He has been raised just as he said" (Matthew); "Why do you search for the living one among the dead? He is not here, but he has been raised " (Luke). Like the women on that first Easter night, we come also in our Easter Vigil to the tomb of Christ and receive the good news of his resurrection.

The Homily

The homily concludes the rite of the Liturgy of the Word by summing up the great and wonderful things God has done for his people and applying these lessons of God's love to the particular group that has assembled to hear the good news of the Easter mystery.

3. The Liturgy of Baptism

The third part of the Easter Vigil Service is the liturgy of baptism. It is in baptism that the light of Christ is first given to us; hence, this sacrament was frequently called "illumination" in the early centuries of the Church, especially in the Eastern Church. Through holy baptism, as we heard in the Epistle Reading, we die to sin and rise with Christ, going down into the font in death in order to come up cleansed from sin and alive unto God.

a) The Liturgy of the Saints

If there are candidates to be baptized or the font to be blessed, the celebrant invites all present to join in praying the Litany of the Saints for those about to receive the "waters of rebirth." By baptism we enter the communion of saints, and so we ask our saintly brothers and sisters to assist and strengthen in faith all those being baptized throughout the world on this night, especially those in our particular parish.

b) The Blessing of the Baptismal Water or Blessing of the Font

The celebrant then blesses the baptismal water or the baptismal font. The blessing prayer for the baptismal water contains a beautiful "theology of water," spelling out the rich symbolism of water in the sacrament of baptism. (The revised text, however, is not as detailed and thorough as the older text was.) The waters that were breathed on by the Spirit at the dawn of creation, the waters of the great flood at the time of Noah, the waters of the Red Sea, the waters of the Jordan in which Christ was baptized, the water and blood that flowed from the side of Christ as he hung upon the cross — the symbolism of all these "waters" in reference to baptism is spelled out in the prayer of blessing.

Then, as the prayer continues, the priest asks the heavenly

Father to unseal the fountain of baptism and to send the grace of the Son and the Holy Spirit upon the waters of the font, so that all who are buried with Christ in the death of baptism might also rise with him to newness of life. (The symbolism of the baptismal font as the womb of Mother Church, bringing forth new children of God, is no longer much in evidence in the revised form of the blessing of the water and font. The plunging of the Easter candle into the water, symbolic of Christ giving the power of life and generation to the womb of Mother Church, is also optional in the revised rite.)

c) Renewal of Baptismal Promises

Following the rite of baptism (and confirmation if administered) or the blessing of the baptismal water if there has been no baptism, is the renewal of the baptismal profession of faith. In this rite we recall our own baptism when, through water and the Holy Spirit, we first died to sin and rose with Christ. We all light our candles for this ceremony, and, with the light of Christ in our hands, we pledge again to reject Satan and sin and all the glamour of evil (dead to sin) and "to serve God faithfully in his holy Catholic Church" (alive to God).

When the priest sprinkles the people with the blessed water as a sacramental renewal of baptism, all should receive the water with sincere sorrow for past sins and with a determination to live in the future as true sons and daughters of God, new men and women who have put on Christ Jesus!

4. The Liturgy of the Eucharist

The Easter Vigil comes to a close with the Liturgy of the Eucharist. By baptism we were made sharers in the saving death and resurrection of Christ. But baptism leads to the Eucharist, the sacrificial reenactment of that death and resurrection of Christ.

As baptized Christians, we not only recall on this night in a solemn way the Passover of Christ from death to resurrection, but we sacramentally relive Christ's Passover deliverance of humankind. For in the eucharistic, sacrificial meal we eat the true paschal Lamb who takes away the sins of the world; we take possession of the resurrected body of the Savior and receive divine life from the victim of Calvary, transformed by God in the resurrection. Christ's passage from death to life now becomes ours as we become the resurrected body of Christ. In the Eucharist we surrender ourselves to Christ and thus die with Christ in order to be clothed with Christ, to be permeated with divine life and power of his resurrected body and blood, with which we now are nourished.

And as we feast upon the flesh and blood of the resurrected victim in the Christian Passover celebration, we are ourselves being resurrected little by little until we are ready for the fullest participation in the unending heavenly banquet of the Father. St. Paul had this vision before him when he wrote this Easter challenge: "If then you were raised with Christ, seek what is above, where Christ is seated at the right hand of God. Think of what is above, not of what is on earth. For you have died, and your life is hidden with Christ in God. When Christ your life appears, then you too will appear with him in glory" (Colossians 3, 1-4).

* * * * * * *

CHAPTER SEVEN

'THE PRINCE OF LIFE, WHO DIED, REIGNS IMMORTAL'

(Sequence of Easter Mass)

The Easter Celebration

AT THE BEGINNING of Chapter Five we spoke of the Easter Cycle as a whole and its various parts, which we said we would treat in three separate chapters: one chapter on Lent; another on Holy Week, with the Easter Triduum; and the third on the remainder of the Easter Cycle, the fifty-day period from Easter Sunday until Pentecost. We are entitling these fifty days "The Easter Celebration."

The Greatness of the Easter Celebration

Father Parsch writes the following words as an introduction to the fifty-day celebration of Easter:

> The mountain is climbed, the victory is achieved. What we have yearned for in the forty anxious days of Lent; indeed, what has been dangling before us as our goal during Advent, today has be-

come a reality: THE LIGHT HAS TRIUMPHED OVER THE DARKNESS! The divine sun of grace now streams down on us with its warming and enlightening rays. In Advent, it was night and we longed eagerly for the light. At Christmas the Light suddenly came into this world and established his kingdom of light, and the glory of this light arose over the holy city (the Church). That was the good news or glad proclamation of the Christmas Cycle. Yet already in the midst of this jubilant leitmotif sounded a foreboding note which became stronger and stronger: "And the light shone in the darkness, but the darkness did not comprehend it" (the suffering motif). This suffering motif was heard already in the octave of Christmas and has not been muted since. Yes, the light did have to go down and set; Christ had to die on the cross. But just as suddenly and abruptly as the light shone in the darkness at Christmas, so now after the sorrow of Holy Week, the Easter sun rises triumphantly to shine for all eternity. That is Easter, the feast of all feasts, the pinnacle of the liturgical year. It calls for one response: loud and lasting jubilation![1]

The Easter celebration commemorates the passover or paschal mystery of Christ and his people. It is the Celebration of Christ's passover from death to new and unending life and our sharing in this passage of Christ through the sacraments, especially the sacrament of baptism, which is *the* Easter sacrament. As St. Paul says, "[We] were baptized into his death . . . we were indeed buried with him through baptism into death, so that, just as Christ was raised from the dead by the glory of the Father, we too might live in newness of life" (Romans 6, 3-4).

This new life is the core of the Easter celebration: the new life of Christ risen from the tomb, the new life granted to Christians through baptism and the other sacraments, and the new life of all creation. Not only did God begin his work of creation on the first day of the week, Sunday. For Christians this day would henceforth be considered not only the first day of the week but also the "eighth day," a day that in a sense falls out-

116

side the system of the week.[2] On this day Jesus conquers sin and death and rises to new life, and we are made new creatures in him with the rest of the created order. This is indeed "the day the Lord has made; let us rejoice and be glad!" (Responsorial Verse of the Easter Mass).

The Little Easter Octave

The first eight days of this fifty-day period of the Easter celebration might be called the "Little Easter Octave" in contrast to the "Great Octave" of seven weeks until Pentecost. The little Easter octave has been marked by special liturgical celebrations since the early part of the fourth century, or perhaps since the second half of the third century.

Today the liturgy of the little Easter octave is seen as a single celebration, in which the Church continues to proclaim each day: "This is the day the Lord has made; let us rejoice and be glad!" (Gospel Acclamation for each day of the octave)

Throughout this little octave, witness after witness comes forward in the Scripture readings of the Masses to give his or her testimony concerning the appearances of the risen Lord. On Monday, it is Peter, the chief of the apostles (First Reading) and the women at the tomb (Gospel) who testify concerning the resurrection of Jesus. On Tuesday, Mary Magdalene announces that she has seen the Lord. On Wednesday, the disciples who walked with Jesus on the road to Emmaus tell how they recognized the risen Lord in the breaking of the bread. On Thursday, we read St. Luke's account of the first appearance of Christ to the disciples on the evening of the resurrection. On Friday, John the Evangelist gives his account of Jesus' appearance to the apostles by the lake, where Jesus prepares their breakfast for them. On Saturday, Mark's Gospel selection for the day sums up all the appearances of Christ since his resurrection. And on Sunday, the last day of the little octave, we hear of the appearance of Christ to the twelve one week after he had risen. On this occasion Thomas is instructed to examine the risen Lord's hands and side. After his response, "My Lord and my God," Jesus added: "Have you come to believe because you have seen me? Blessed are they who have not seen and have believed" (John 20, 28-29). Those last words of Jesus draw us into the group of those who believe in the risen Lord and who are to be witnesses to him.

The Great Octave of Seven Weeks

But not only is the little octave considered as a single feast and celebration; the whole fifty-day period from Easter Sunday until Pentecost is celebrated as one feast by the Church. We find this fact stated in the new *General Norms for the Liturgical Year*, where we read that "the fifty days from Easter Sunday to Pentecost are celebrated as one feast day, sometimes called 'the great Sunday' " (n. 22). In the early Church this fifty-day feast was characterized by joyous thanksgiving that found expression, among other ways, in frequent alleluias and a prohibition against fasting and against kneeling for prayer.[3]

Throughout this fifty-day feast day the Easter candle, which is the outstanding symbol of the risen Lord, remains in the sanctuary and is lit during the liturgy each day as a visual sign of the unity of these days. (At an earlier time it was customary to extinguish the Easter candle and remove it after the Gospel was read on the Feast of the Ascension.)

Another change since Vatican II that brings out the unity of the Easter season or celebration is to call the Sundays that fall in this period not "the Sundays *after* Easter," but "the Sundays *of* Easter." And throughout the seven weeks of the Easter celebration, the liturgy almost constantly focuses on the prayers and readings on the resurrection of Christ and his continued dwelling among us.

The Scripture Readings During the Easter Celebration

It is a little difficult to sum up adequately in a short space all the Scripture readings that are presented in the Sunday and

118

Weekday Lectionary during the fifty days of the Easter celebration.

The first readings of the three cycles for the Sundays of Easter are all taken from the Acts of the Apostles and present the witness of Peter and Paul to the resurrection of Christ and the effects of this belief in the resurrection in the early days and years of the Church. The second readings of the Sundays of Easter are either from the First Letter of Peter (Cycle A), the First Letter of John (Cycle B) or the Book of Revelation (Cycle C), whose authors speak about the crucified and risen Christ and his meaning and relationship to the Christian people. The Gospels of these Sundays (almost all from John, except on the third Sunday of Easter) narrate some of the appearances of the risen Christ (third Sunday); present Christ as the Good Shepherd (fourth Sunday), and as the Way, Truth, and Life or the True Vine (fifth Sunday); or they offer excerpts from the Last Discourse or High-Priestly Prayer of Jesus in chapters 14 to 17 of John's Gospel (sixth and seventh Sundays).

The first reading of the Weekday Lectionary of the seven weeks of Easter are also all from the Acts of the Apostles (chapters 4 through 28), while the Gospel selections are all from the Gospel of John and center in on the discourses of Christ on new birth (Nicodemus), the bread of life, the good shepherd, and the last discourse of Jesus to his apostles concerning his kingdom, its law of love, and the sending of the Spirit.

The Feast of the Ascension

The Feast of the Ascension of the Lord is celebrated forty days after Easter (or in some countries on the following Sunday). It is a feast closely related to the resurrection and in many ways an extension of it, since the ascension of Christ into heaven completes the upward swing of Christ's exaltation that began with his resurrection after he had humbled himself to death on a cross.

This feast is a joyful and triumphal feast and lacks any tone of sadness over the fact that Christ in his human form has departed from us. (For he still remains with us in other ways). It is a feast of triumph inasmuch as Christ has now completed his task here on earth and is now seated in glory at the right hand of his Father in heaven until he will come again at the end of time. As the Second Reading for this feast proclaims: "He put all things under his [Christ's] feet and gave him as head over all things to the Church, which is his body; the fullness of the one who fills all things in every way" (Ephesians 1, 22-23).

But this feast is also a day of joy and triumph for us because the glorification of Christ in his ascension is also the elevation of the human nature which Christ had assumed. Hence, we celebrate not only Christ's glorification but also our glorification. One of our own is seated at the right hand of the Father as a true intermediary and intercessor for us, partaking in the highest divine honor.

The Fathers of the Church grasped that idea profoundly and wrote of it frequently. St. Leo the Great, for example, writes in a sermon for the Ascension:

> The ascension of Christ thus means our own elevation as well; where the glorious Head has gone before, the Body is called to follow in hope. Let us therefore exult, beloved, as is fitting, and let us rejoice in devout thanksgiving. For on this day not only have we been confirmed in our possession of paradise, but we have entered heaven in the person of Christ; through his ineffable grace we have regained far more than we lost through the devil's hatred.[4]

Thus, the Feast of the Ascension of Christ is not just a celebration of a historical event in the life of Jesus but a celebration of what we ourselves now are and are called to be. The first preface for this feast can therefore proclaim: "Christ the mediator between God and man, judge of the world and Lord of all, has passed beyond our sight, not to abandon us but to be our hope. Christ is the beginning, the head of the Church; where he has gone we hope to follow."

The Feast of Pentecost

The feast that now closes the Easter season on the fiftieth day of Easter is the Feast of Pentecost, which word means "fifty." Although there is a kind of liturgical novena leading up to Pentecost, there is no longer an octave of Pentecost or a season of Sundays after Pentecost.

Pentecost is also no longer seen in the liturgy as a separate feast of the Holy Spirit, but rather as the fulfillment and completion of the resurrection. The Opening Prayer of the Pentecost Mass brings out that connection between Easter and Pentecost: "Almighty and ever-living God, you fulfilled the Easter promise by sending us your Holy Spirit." And the new preface for Pentecost likewise stresses the close connection of Easter and Pentecost in these words: "Today you send the Holy Spirit on those marked to be your children by sharing the life of your only Son, and so you brought the paschal mystery to its completion. . . The joy of the resurrection renews the whole world, while the choirs of heaven sing for ever to your glory."

Already in the Old Testament there was a feast of Pentecost or "feast of weeks" which was celebrated fifty days after the feast of Unleavened Bread. This Jewish Feast of Weeks or Pentecost was a feast of thanksgiving for the wheat harvest and a memorial of the establishment of the covenant between God and his people on Mt. Sinai. That Jewish feast thus becomes the forerunner of the Christian feast of Pentecost which establishes a new covenant with the followers of Jesus, who as the new "people of God" give thanks for the harvest of souls that the Spirit has begun in the Church. The work of harvesting begun by Christ will be carried on in the Church by the Spirit.

Pentecost celebrates then the great outpouring of the Spirit of Jesus and the Father on the disciples as they gathered in the Upper Room in Jerusalem. In one of his sermons, Pope St. Leo insists that this was not the first outpouring of the Holy Spirit, for he had already been given to the patriarchs and prophets and priests and saints of earlier times. On Pentecost, however, says Leo, the Spirit was poured out in a far greater measure than ever before.[5]

That Spirit who was given at Pentecost and before Pentecost also continues to be given after Pentecost. He continues to act in the guidance of the Church; he continues to inspire and strengthen the faith of the present-day disciples of Christ through the sacraments, the Scriptures, and through the prayer that he enables us to offer to the Father.

And so we pray:

Father of light, from whom every good gift comes,
send your Spirit into our lives with the power of a mighty wind;
and by the flame of your wisdom open the horizons of our minds.
Loosen our tongue to sing your praise in words beyond the power of speech,
for without your Spirit we could never raise our voices in words of peace or announce the truth that Jesus is Lord,
who lives and reigns with you and the Holy Spirit, one God, for ever and ever. Amen.

(Alternate Prayer for Pentecost)

* * * * * * *

CHAPTER EIGHT

'OUR VOICES IN HIM AND HIS VOICE IN US'

(St. Augustine)

The Liturgy of the Hours

WE CONCLUDE our study and reflection on the liturgical year with a chapter on the Liturgy of the Hours (the Divine Office), which is the official public prayer of the Church especially, but not exclusively, for the clergy and Religious of the Church. In this official daily prayer of the Church we find another of the ways that Christ fulfills his promise: "Behold, I am with you always, until the end of the age" (Matthew 28, 27).

The Constitution on the Sacred Liturgy and the Divine Office

Chapter Four of the *Constitution on the Sacred Liturgy*, the first document promulgated by the Second Vatican Council, is devoted to the Divine Office, more commonly called today "The Liturgy of the Hours." The opening paragraphs of that Chapter Four give a beautiful summary of the meaning and importance of this public prayer of the Church and the relationship with Christ that the recital of this prayer entail. We quote:

> Christ Jesus, high priest of the new and eternal covenant, taking human nature, introduced into this earthly exile that hymn which is sung throughout all ages in the halls of heaven. He joins the entire community of mankind to himself, associating it with his own singing of this canticle of divine praise.
>
> For he continues his priestly work through the agency of his Church, which is ceaselessly engaged in praising the Lord and interceding for the salvaton of the whole world. She does this, not only by celebrating the Eucharist, but also in other ways, especially by praying the divine office.
>
> By a tradition going back to early Christian times, the divine office is devised so that the whole course of the day and night is made holy by the praises of God. Therefore, when this wonderful song of praise is rightly performed by priests and others who are deputed for this purpose by the Church's ordinance, or by the faithful praying together with the priest in the approved form, then it is truly the voice of the bride addressed to her bridegroom; it is the very prayer which Christ himself, together with his body, addresses to the Father.
>
> Hence all who render this service are not only fulfilling a duty of the Church, but also are sharing in the greatest honor of Christ's spouse, for by offering these praises to God they are standing before God's throne in the name of the Church their Mother (n. 83-85).

The General Instruction on the Liturgy of the Hours

After the close of the Second Vatican Council a commission was set up to carry out the reform or "restoration" of the Divine Office that had been decreed in the *Constitution on the Liturgy* (cf. nn. 87-101). This commission worked for almost seven years before the final version of the restored Liturgy of the Hours was published in 1970. But several years prior to the completed publication of all the revised texts, the commission published in 1967 what is known as the *General Instruction on the Liturgy of the Hours*. One liturgist has called this general instruction "a remarkable document," with which judgment I personally agree. The document is not just a rubric book on how to pray the Divine Office, but includes a succinct yet profound treatment of the theological basis for praying the Divine Office as a whole and in its individual parts.

The remainder of this chapter will be based heavily on the *General Instruction on the Liturgy of the Hours* as we consider (a) some of the theological principles that underlie and give meaning to the praying of the Liturgy of the Hours, and (b) the spirit of the individual hours of the Divine Office.

The Theology of the Liturgy of the Hours

By "theology of the Liturgy of the Hours" is meant the theological truths or spiritual principles which offer meaning and purpose and value to the praying of the Divine Office. Our treatment will not claim to be an exhaustive one, but will cover, I believe, the most important and inspiring of these theological truths that are associated with the praying of the Liturgy of the Hours.

1. When We Pray the Liturgy of the Hours, We Join in the Prayer of Christ, the God-man

The first of these theological truths or principles is also probably the most profound and important. Yet, at the same time, it can be stated rather simply: When we pray the Liturgy of the Hours, we join in the prayer of Christ, the God-man.

The principle is contained and expressed quite cogently in the words from the *Constitution on the Liturgy* quoted above (n. 83). The last line of paragraph No. 84 adds that the Liturgy of the Hours "is the very prayer which Christ himself, together with his body, addresses to the Father."

We know that Christ, the Son of God, who took on our human

nature, was a person of great prayer. As our High Priest and mediator with the Father, he has introduced into the world the praise of the Father. And in Christ, the God-become-flesh, the praise of the Father finds the most perfect expression in human words and gestures and feelings and thoughts.

This Jesus Christ, Son of God and Son of Mary, not only prayed while he was on this earth in human form, but he continues to pray to the Father and to intercede for us in heaven. He prays in the name of all people and for the good of all people.

We, as members of the Church, have the duty and privilege of praying, asking, and seeking as Christ commands us to do in his name. In a particular way, says the *Constitution on the Liturgy*, we carry out that command in the Liturgy of the Hours, the official public prayer of the Church (n. 83). We, the members of the Church, continue and join in the prayer that Christ "introduced into this earthly exile." We continue to pray with our human voice, gestures, thoughts, and feelings to the Father as did Christ. We continue to pray many of the same psalms and prayers that Christ himself prayed. We continue to pray with the same human emotions that filled the heart of Christ as he praised and thanked his Father, as he interceded and petitioned his Father for various favors for himself and others, and as he sought forgiveness and mercy for sins, though he himself never sinned.

The *General Instruction on the Liturgy of the Hours* quotes a beautiful section from St. Augustine that emphasizes this point:

> God could present no greater gift to human beings than to make his Word, through whom he created all things, their Head, so that they might in like manner be his members. His Word is Son of God and Son of Man, one God with the Father, one Man with human beings. When we speak to God in prayer, the Son is not separated from the Father, and when the Son's Body prays, the Head is not separated from the Body. It is the *one* Savior of his own

Body, our Lord Jesus Christ, the Son of God, who *prays for us, prays in us,* and is *prayed to by us.* He prays in us as our Head, he prays for us as our Priest, and he is prayed to by us as our God. Let us, therefore, recognize our voices in him and his voice in us.

The *General Instruction* adds this further comment: "The dignity of Christian prayer, therefore, derives from the fact that it participates in the filial piety of the only-begotten Son toward the Father and in his prayer which, in his earthly life, he expressed in words in the name of the whole human race and for the salvation of mankind, and which he continues to express in the whole Church and in her members" (n. 7).

2. When We Pray the Liturgy of the Hours, We Are United With All the Angels and Saints in Heaven

We are not only united with Christ in the praying of the Liturgy of the Hours, but also united with all the angels and saints in heaven as they voice the canticle of praise which is sung throughout all the ages in the halls of heaven.

We are united with Mary, who by the privilege of her assumption, is also bodily in heaven with her Son. We are united with our favorite saints and all the saints from every tribe and tongue and people and nation, who, though still awaiting the glorification of their bodies, stand before the throne of God, as described in the Book of Revelation, and cry out their praise to God (cf. Revelation 7, 9-10). Among these saints are likewise many of our relatives and friends who have passed away. With this whole Church triumphant in heaven, we magnify with one song of praise the one and triune God (*Constitution on the Church,* n. 50).

In praying the Divine Office we also unite ourselves with the choirs of angels who surround the throne of God and continuously, as Isaiah describes it (Isaiah 6, 3), sing: "Holy, holy, holy is the Lord of hosts! . . . All the earth is filled with his glory!" Because of the transcendence of the angels over matter, Scripture and tradition have attributed to them the special task of praising God. Of them St. Basilius says: "To glorify God is the office of the angels. This is the duty of the whole celestial army, namely, to give glory to the Creator."[1] St. Gregory of Nyssa offers these thoughts:

> The angels, too, teach us to forget our human nature when we are praying, and how not to consider present things, but rather to imagine ourselves in their midst, and to offer the same worship they do. True, they differ from us in nature, way of life, wisdom, comprehension, and in many other ways; but prayer is something which we have in common with them. As far as prayer is concerned, there is no difference between us. Prayer separates us from irrational animals but it unites us with the angels. The person who devotes himself to prayer and to worship is elevated to citizenship, the way of life, the dignity, the nobility, the wisdom and the comprehension of the angels.[2]

The prayer of the Liturgy of the Hours, in which we are united with Christ and all the saints and angels in heaven, becomes, as does the Mass, "a foretaste of the heavenly praise sung unceasingly before the throne of God and of the Lamb, as described by John in the Book of Revelations" (GI, n. 16). In this sense, says one author, the Liturgy of the Hours is "a preview of coming attractions."[3] It keeps before our eyes the fact that our life on earth is fleeting and passing and the hope of a better life to come, a life of eternal joy in the companionship of a God who is eternal love and of all the angels and blessed in heaven.

3. When We Pray the Liturgy of the Hours, We Represent the Church, All Mankind, and All Creation

A third theological principle that is connected with the praying of the Liturgy of the Hours is that when we pray the Liturgy of the Hours, we are representatives of the whole Church, of all mankind, and of all creation.

The basis of this particular truth is the first principle, which we have already explained in some detail. Because our voice of prayer in the Liturgy of the Hours is united with the prayer of Christ, this prayer is also united with the whole body of Christ, the Church, and with the whole of creation through the King and Lord of creation. The *General Instruction* in nn. 7 and 8 speaks of this union between Christ and creation and Christ and the Church in these words: "For Christ so unites the whole community of mankind to himself that there is an intimate and necessary relationship between the prayer of Christ and the prayer of the whole human race. . . . A special and most intimate bond, however, exists between Christ and those whom he makes members of his Body, the Church, through the sacrament of regeneration."

What follows from this is that when we pray the Liturgy of the Hours, or take part in other liturgical functions such as the Mass and the sacraments, we are taking part not in just a private function but one that pertains to the whole body of the Church. This is so even if the Liturgy of the Hours were to be recited quietly and in solitude by a single individual. In such a situation, this praying of the Divine Office remains the public prayer of the Church, for in such a situation persons praying the Liturgy of the Hours are not truly alone; Christ is with these persons, uniting their prayers as one; and the whole Church is with these persons, praying and being prayed for.

It is, of course, much better if we pray this "community" prayer of the Church in a community, that is, with others. And the more and better diversified the group is, the better such a community of prayers will bring out the communal nature of the Church and this public prayer of the Church. The *General Instruction* says with regard to this ideal of praying the Liturgy of the Hours with others: "Celebration in common shows more clearly the ecclesial (community) nature of the Liturgy of the Hours" (n. 33). The private recitation of the Divine Office, though it became at times the more normal practice in the

Church, was never considered by the Church as normal and still less as ideal. By reciting the Liturgy of the Hours privately, the priest or religious or layperson is simply making up for the fact that he or she is not able to celebrate the Divine Office in common with others.

Thus, the Liturgy of the Hours is the public and communal prayer of the Church as it manifests this Church and also has an effect upon this Church (cf. *General Instruction*, n. 20). Hence, when we pray this official community prayer of the Church, we represent the Church and are the Church. We cause the universal Church to be present; we pray in its name and carry out one of the main duties of the Church, which is "to pray continually and never lose heart" (Luke 18, 1; cf. *GI*, n. 28). "All who take part in the Divine Office are not only performing a duty for the Church, they are also sharing in what is the greatest honor for Christ's Bride, for by offering these praises to God they are standing before God's throne in the name of the Church, their Mother" (*Constitution on the Liturgy*, n. 85).

I would like to add a few thoughts on how we are also representatives of the whole human race, not just the baptized members of Christ's Church, in our praying of the Liturgy of the Hours. Generally when we think of the "Church," we are thinking of the Roman Catholic Church, and indeed the Church of Christ or the Body of Christ does "subsist in the Catholic Church," as the *Constitution on the Church* of Vatican II has stated (n. 8). Yet, that same document proclaims that "all men and women are called to be part of this catholic unity of the people of God . . . and they belong to or are related to it in various ways, the Catholic faithful, all who believe in Christ, and indeed the whole of mankind, for all men and women are called by the grace of God to salvation" (n. 13).

Therefore, when we pray the Liturgy of the Hours, we should not just limit thinking of ourselves as the official representatives of the Roman Catholic Church, but should see ourselves as the representatives of all the human race, whether

Catholics or Protestants or Muslims or Buddhists or pagans or atheists. We stand before God in our prayer as representatives of all men and women who live in our world today.

We are representatives too of all the animal and plant world and of the whole inanimate creation. A number of the psalms and canticles that we use in the Liturgy of the Hours have the frame of mind that all of creation in its own way gives praise to God and we join with them in this praise. The Canticle of the Three Young Men, Psalm 66, Psalm 96, Psalm 148, and Psalm 150 are a few of the prayers that we use in the Divine Office which specifically call on all created things to give praise and thanks to their Creator. These animals and plants and other inanimate creatures cannot, of course, give knowing and willful praise and glory to God, for they cannot know and reflect and believe that there is a God and that he is their Creator, deserving of their praise and glory. Gerard Manley Hopkins writes in this connection:

> The sun and the stars shining glorify God. They stand where he placed them, they move where he bid them. 'The heavens declare the glory of God.' They glorify God, *but they do not know it.* The birds sing to him, the thunder speaks of his terror, the lion is like his strength, the sea is like his greatness, the honey like his sweetness; they are something like him, they make him known, they tell of him, they give him glory, but they do not know they do, they do not know him, they never can, they are brute things that only think of food or think of nothing. This then is poor praise, faint reverence, slight service, dull glory. Nevertheless, what they can *they always do.*[4]

We human beings, however, with our gifts of intellect and free will, can know and believe in God and knowingly and freely offer him praise and glory in behalf of and as representatives of all creation. And we are made for this, as Hopkins concludes in the work quoted above:

But amidst them all is man, man and the angels: we will speak of man. Man was created. Like the rest then to praise, reverence, and serve God; to give him glory. He does so even by his being beyond all visible creatures. . . . But man can know God, *can mean to give him glory*. This then was why he was made, to give God glory and to mean to give it; to praise God freely, willingly to reverence him, gladly to serve him. Man was made to give, and *mean* to give, God glory. I was made for this, each one of us was made for this.

To sum up this third theological principle related to the praying of the Liturgy of the Hours: In the Liturgy of the Hours we become united with Jesus our Head and with his Body the Church — and through them with all of mankind and all of creation. We become one with the hungry child, the lonely grandmother, the worker in the field and factory; we become one with the addict and the alcoholic, the hardworking housewife and searching young student; we become one with the atheist, the communist, the criminal in jail, the child in the school, the dying in the hospital; we become one with the birds and the beavers, the stars and the stones. We become in our praying of the Liturgy of the Hours the voice and spokesperson for all creation, singing out to the Father in joyful adoration and praise and thanks, but also crying to him for mercy and forgiveness and help in our need and distress.

4. When We Pray the Liturgy of the Hours, We Consecrate the Time of Each Day

The fourth and last theological principle that we will consider in relation to the praying of the Liturgy of the Hours is that when we pray the Divine Office, we consecrate the course of each day or the time of each day. The *General Instruction* speaks of this aspect of the Liturgy of the Hours in this fashion:

Christ taught us the necessity of praying at all times without losing heart (Luke 18, 1). The Church has been faithful in obeying this instruction; it never ceases to offer prayer, and makes this exhortation its own: "Through him [Jesus] let us offer to God an unceasing sacrifice of praise" (Hebrews 1, 15). The Church satisfies this requirement not only by the celebration of the Eucharist but in other ways also, especially through the Liturgy of the Hours, which is distinguished from other liturgical actions by the fact that it consecrates to God the whole cycle of day and night, as it has done from early Christian times.

Since the purpose of the Liturgy of the Hours includes the sanctification of the day and the whole range of human activity, its structure has been revised in such a way that, as far as possible, each Hour might be celebrated once more at the proper time and account taken of the circumstances of life today.

Hence, "in order that the day may be truly sanctified and the Hours themselves recited with spiritual profit, it is preferable that they should be recited at the hour nearest to the one indicated by each canonical Hour" (*Constitution on Sacred Liturgy*, n. 88; *GI*, nn. 10 and 11).

I'd like to make the following comments on these paragraphs from the *General Instruction* concerning how the Liturgy of the Hours consecrates the time or hours of each day:

a) First of all, the consecration of the time or whole course of each day and night is the particular characteristic of the Liturgy of the Hours that distinguishes it from other liturgical actions of the Church. The Liturgy of the Hours is meant to consecrate or sanctify by prayer the whole course of the day. The name we now give this public prayer of the Church (Liturgy of the *Hours*) emphasizes this special characteristic of the Divine Office.

b) The Liturgy of the Hours doesn't consecrate time in general or every second of the day (except insofar as somewhere in the world someone is probably praying a part of the Divine Office during every minute of the day). But the way the Liturgy of the Hours consecrates or sanctifies time is by sanctifying certain specific periods of each day: the morning, the evening, the third, sixth, and ninth hours, the time before we go to bed. These are the high points of our day by which we move in the direction of fulfilling the command of Christ to pray always and the exhortation in Hebrews to "offer God an unending sacrifice of praise." The Divine Office cannot, of course, provide us with absolute continual liturgical prayer. Life demands other activities in our life from which the liturgical life cannot exclude us: eating meals, work, study, sleep, leisure activities. But the Hours, if we pray them at the times of the day that they are meant to be prayed, at least moves us in the direction of praying always.

c) Finally, we would like to emphasize here, as the *General Instruction* does, that the individual Hours should be prayed, as far as possible, at the time of day that they are intended to be prayed: morning prayer in the morning; evening prayer in the evening; Compline immediately before going to bed; etc. One of the chief purposes in the revision of the Divine Office was to make it possible that the Hours be genuinely related to the time of day at which they are prayed, and this not only for monastic or cloistered groups of Religious, but for all members of the Church. The *General Instruction* in paragraph n. 11 indicates two important advantages of praying the Hours at the time which corresponds to their true canonical time: the whole day is thus truly sanctified and consecrated; and the Hours can thereby be recited with greater spiritual advantage.

The Spirit of the Individual Hours of the Divine Office

Our final section in this chapter on the Liturgy of the Hours is to consider the spirit of the individual Hours of the Divine Office as we find them in the Church's revised texts of the Liturgy of the Hours. In treating of this "spirit" of the Hours, we will be looking at the particular time or period of the day that each Hour is meant to consecrate and at the themes or mysteries that we celebrate in the individual Hours.

134

1. The Morning Prayer of Lauds

"Lauds is designed and structured," says the *General Instruction*, "to sanctify the morning, as is clear from its parts" (n. 38). The canonical time for the Hours of Lauds is, then, the morning, or more accurately, *the beginning of the day*, daybreak, when the sun is rising and the light of a new day dawns.

The *General Instruction* quotes St. Basil the Great, who indicates what it is of ourselves that we consecrate at the beginning of the day: namely, the first movements or stirrings of our minds and hearts.

The main theme or mystery of the life of Christ that we celebrate in the Hour of Lauds is that of the resurrection of Christ and what follows from that; namely, the continued presence of the risen Christ with us, and the promise and hope of our own resurrection and sharing in Christ's victory and glory. The rising of the sun symbolizes the rising of Christ from the tomb, who is, as the Canticle of Zechariah which we use in this Hour puts it, "the rising sun" or "the dawn from on high that breaks upon us, to shine on those who dwell in darkness and the shadow of death, and to guide our feet into the way of peace." Those words of the Canticle apply very fittingly to the risen Christ, who each day shines on us with the light of his teaching and example and with the light and warmth of his love and mercy; thereby he guides our feet each day into the way of eternal peace.

The word "Lauds" means "praises," and so this hour is also characterized especially by psalms and hymns of praise to God our Creator and Redeemer and Lord. Prayer of praise is "essentially an unlimited appreciation of the grandeur of God, a loving appreciation which expresses itself in words, and better still in song. It is not a cold and objective statement, but warm and human acknowledgment of God."[5] Such prayer of praise is our acknowledgment and appreciation of the greatness and goodness of God who alone is all-good, almighty, all-wise, and all-merciful.

Finally, we should mention that the Hours of Lauds often

has missionary overtones. It is an Hour that challenges us to spread the Gospel of Christ to all the nations as the risen Christ commissioned his disciples to do before he ascended into heaven. Like John the Baptist in the Canticle of Zechariah, we are called "to go before the Lord to prepare his way." We should consider these words of Zechariah to his son John as being addressed to us each morning by our heavenly Father: "You, my child, shall be called the prophet of the Most High; for you will go before the Lord to prepare his way, to give his people knowledge of salvation by the forgiveness of sin."

2. The Hour of Vespers

There are two hinges or principal Hours "on which the daily Office turns," says the *General Instruction* (n. 37). The first hinge is Lauds or Morning Prayer and the other hinge is Vespers. "They are to be considered as the chief hours," says the *General Instruction*, "and are to be celebrated as such."

The canonical time to be consecrated by Vespers is the evening, or again more specifically, "when the day is drawing to a close," as the sun is setting (n. 39). The word "Vespers" comes from the Latin word that means "evening."

The main theme of Lauds was the Resurrection, and the main theme we recall and celebrate at Vespers is the redemption by Christ which was accomplished through Christ's offering of himself for us. This sacrifice of Christ was his evening sacrifice which he celebrated in sacramental form with his apostles in the evening of his passion and which he completed the following day "by the raising up of his hands for the salvation of the whole world" on the cross (n. 39). Thus we join ourselves with Christ in his evening sacrifice as we offer ourselves with him in our evening sacrifice of praise. These themes of the redemption of Christ and the evening sacrifice, which was celebrated by the Jews at this hour, are found in many of the psalms and canticles used in Vespers. Practically all the New Testament canticles used on the various days of the week speak of Christ's redemption, and many psalms speak of offering a sacrifice to God.

The predominant type of prayer in Lauds was prayer of praise. The predominant type of prayer in Vespers is thanksgiving. "While praise considers God in himself, thanksgiving considers him in relation to us. . . . He is God for us. . . . We thank God for all that he has given us: not only for everything that we have, but for what we are. We thank him for all that exists, and therefore for himself above all."[6] So we give thanks to God in this Hour as the day is drawing to a close "for what has been given us during the day, or for the things we have done well during it," as the *General Instruction* states (n. 39). Many of the psalms used in this Hour of Vespers will be thanksgiving psalms, and every day we pray or sing Mary's Canticle of Thanks, the Magnificat. This song of Mary is considered the high point of the Vespers celebration. It is one of the most exalted expressions of joyous thanks that we have, and in this Magnificat we join then with Mary in giving thanks to God and we make her expression of thanks that of the Church and of ourselves as individuals. We give thanks that God has this day "looked with favor on me" and the Church; that he "has done great things for me" today; that he has bestowed his mercy on all those "who fear him." We thank God in Mary's words that "he has helped Israel his servant" the new Israel his Church, for this day "he has remembered his promise of mercy."

3. The Middle Hour (Hours of Terce, Sext, and None)

The Hours of Terce, Sext, and None are still retained in the Liturgy of the Hours for those who lead a contemplative life, and they are recommended for everyone, especially in times of retreat or pastoral gatherings (n. 76). If these Hours are said, however, they should be said at the corresponding canonical time and not lumped together into one block of prayer. It was precisely to avoid this lumping of Hours together that the Middle Hour or Daytime Prayer was introduced.

The canonical times to be consecrated by these "small"

Hours are traditionally the third, sixth and ninth hours of the day as their names indicate (9 A.M., 12 noon, and 3 P.M.). The person who is just saying the Middle Hour simply chooses the small Hour that corresponds most suitably to the actual time that the Middle Hour is being celebrated.

The temporal characteristic of this Middle Hour, as the name in English indicates, is that it comes in the middle of or between the Morning Lauds and Evening Vespers. The prayers of the Middle Hour and of all the small Hours is to offer the opportunity of a breathing space in God's presence while we are in the midst of our work or other activity. It also helps to sanctify this work or activity without interrupting it too much. Thus, this prayer is an effort to imitate the Apostolic Church, says the *General Instruction*, who "from the earliest times . . . even in the midst of their work, dedicated various moments to prayer throughout the course of the day" (n. 74).

There are particular themes that are related to each of the small Hours. These themes for the most part stem from events in the life of Christ or in the Church that occurred at these times of day and related in the Scriptures as occurring at these specific hours.

a) *Terce:* Terce is the Hour of the Holy Spirit because it is thought that the coming of the Holy Spirit on Pentecost took place near the third hour. We have Peter's words in Acts: "These men are not drunk, as you suppose, for it is only nine o'clock in the morning [the third hour of the day]" (2, 15). It is fitting, then, that we sing a hymn to the Holy Spirit at the Hour of Terce.

b) *Sext:* It is hard to characterize precisely the Hour of Sext. I prefer to call it "the Hour of salvation for the Gentiles" in view of the fact that it was at the sixth hour, noontime, according to Acts 10, 9, that Peter was praying and was hungry and had the vision of the sheet filled with clean and unclean foods which symbolized the entry of the Gentile world into the Church of Christ.

At this sixth hour, Jesus is also thought to have ascended to heaven, having given his disciples the commission to preach the Gospel to all the world.

Another event that John records as taking place "about noon [the sixth hour]" (John 19, 14) was Jesus' appearance before Pilate and the rejection of Jesus by his people. "We have no King but Caesar," they cried out. "Then he handed him over to be crucified" (John 19, 15-16).

c) *None:* I believe that the death of Christ, which according to Matthew and Mark took place "at the ninth hour," should be the main theme of this small Hour of None. Another event that took place at the ninth hour was the healing of the cripple at the Beautiful Gate by Peter and John as they went up to the temple for prayers at the ninth hour (Acts 3, 1).

4. The Hour of Compline or Night Prayer

The Hour of Compline is described by the *General Instruction* as "the final prayer of the day to be said before going to bed," and the "before" has the meaning of "just before" or "soon before," and not two or three hours before. This Hour consecrates the last acts of our day. The name "Compline," from the Latin word *completorium*, means the prayers that complete and conclude our day. The *General Instruction* says: "Compline is the final prayer of the day to be said before going to bed, even if this is after midnight" (n. 84). In other words, the instruction prefers that this Hour be said right before going to bed rather than before midnight during the actual day that is prescribed, if one doesn't go to bed before midnight. Before the revised Divine Office, it was mandatory to pray Compline before midnight even if you intended to stay up later.

Inasmuch as this Hour encourages an examination of conscience and penitential prayers (n. 86), this Hour is characterized in one way by contrition and sorrow for faults committed during the day. Since many of the psalms chosen for this Hour are psalms of trust and confidence in God, we can also characterize the Hour of Compline as a prayer of trust in God. But the predominant element of this Hour is the commending of our lives into God's hands during the hours of sleep. We find this theme expressed in the Responsory used each night: "Into your hands, I commend my spirit"; also in the Canticle of Simeon, which canticle the *General Instruction* calls "the culmination of the whole Hour" (n. 89). Like Simeon, full of thanks for all the workings and manifestations of God in our lives this day, we are prepared to leave the world if God wishes it, and we commend ourselves into his loving and provident care.

5. The Office of Readings

The Office of Readings, as this part of the Divine Office is now called, corresponds to the old "Matins," which was, at least theoretically a night office. The present Office of Readings, however, is no longer characterized as the other Hours by the *time* at which it is to be said. Hence, this part of the Liturgy of the Hours is not strictly an "Hour," and it may be recited, says the *General Instruction*, "at any hour of the day, or even in the night hours of the preceding day, after Vespers" (n. 59).

The *General Instruction* does, however, encourage those who lead a contemplative life and others on special occasions to retain the nocturnal character of the Office of Readings by celebrating it as a Vigil Office (nn. 70-74). If that is done, this Office of Readings would have the spirit of the vigil or night office, which is that of staying awake and looking forward to the Lord's coming at the end of time.

What particularly characterizes the Office of Readings is its *content*: namely, readings from the sacred Scriptures and from the Fathers of the Church and other spiritual authors. Its purpose, says the *General Instruction*, is "to present . . . a more extensive meditation on Sacred Scripture and on the best writings of spiritual authors" (n. 55). This reading and meditation on the Scriptures and other writings is meant, of course, to assist our spiritual progress, to fill us with the food of God's word and spirit, enabling us to impart this word and spirit to others (n. 55).

Though the principal character of the Office of Readings is the actual readings, there are also other prayers connected with this office. There is the Invitatory, a hymn, three psalms, or three divisions of a psalm, and other prayers and formulas. The reasoning behind this, as the *General Instruction* states quite well, is that "Prayer should accompany the reading of sacred Scripture to make it a conversation between God and human beings; we speak to him when we pray and he speaks to us when we read the divine words" (n. 56).

* * * * * * *

We conclude our reflections on the Liturgy of the Hours and on the presence of Christ in our midst throughout the liturgical year with the words of Pope Paul VI in his letter of promulgation of the revised Divine Office. The Pope writes:

> May the praise of God reecho in the Church of our day with greater grandeur and beauty by means of the new Liturgy of the Hours. . . . May it join the praises sung by the saints and angels in the court of heaven. May it go from strength to strength in the days of this earthly exile and soon attain the fullness of praise which will be given throughout eternity "to the one who sits on the throne and to the Lamb" (Revelation 5, 13).

* * * * * * *

CHAPTER NOTES

CHAPTER ONE

1. Pius Parsch, O.S.B., *Das Jahr des Heiles*, Band I (Verlag Volkliturgisches Apostolat, Klosterneuburg b. Wien), p. 11 (author's translation; all quotes from Father Parsch in this book are the author's translation).
2. Adolf Adam, *The Liturgical Year: Its History and Its Meaning After the Reform of the Liturgy* (Pueblo Publishing Company, New York), p. vii.
3. Adam, ibidem, p. vii.
4. Cf. Adam, ibid., p. 19.
5. Pius XII, Encyclical *Mediator Dei*, n. 163.
6. Adam, op. cit., p. 22.
7. Adrian Nocent, O.S.B., *The Liturgical Year*, Vol. 1 (The Liturgical Press, Collegeville, Minn.), p. 16.
8. Nocent, ibid., p. 17.
9. Adam, op. cit., p. 27.

CHAPTER TWO

1. Nocent, op. cit., pp. 67-68.
2. Parsch, op. cit., pp. 28-30. Almost all of this section on "The Heralds of Advent" is based heavily on Parsch.
3. Nocent, op. cit., p. 47.
4. Nocent, op. cit., pp. 32-33.
5. Parsch, op. cit., p. 30.
6. Parsch, op. cit., pp. 31-32.

CHAPTER THREE

1. Cf. Adam, op. cit., p. 121.
2. Cf. Adam, ibid., p. 123.
3. Cf. Parsch, op. cit., p. 236.
4. Cf. Adam, op. cit., p. 125.
5. Adam, ibid., p. 125.

CHAPTER FOUR

1. Eugene Maly, "Council Commentary" in *Cincinnati Catholic Telegraph* (1966).
2. *Constitution on the Liturgy*, n. 106.
3. Jacques D. Migne, *Patrologia Graeca*, Vol. 61, col. 227.

CHAPTER FIVE

1. Nocent, op. cit., Vol. 2, p. 19.
2. Pope St. Leo the Great, *Sermo* 47.
3. Pope St. Leo, *Sermo* 42.
4. St. Augustine, *Sermo* 206.
5. Pope St. Leo, *Sermo* 49.
6. Parsch, op. cit., Band II, pp. 105-106.

CHAPTER SIX

1. Nocent, op. cit., Vol. 2, p. 187-88.
2. Ibid., p. 195.
3. The ideas for the section on "vigil" were drawn chiefly from two books published by the Liturgical Press (Collegeville, Minn.): *The Meaning of Holy Week* by Rev. William J. O'Shea and *Holy Week and Easter* by Dom Jean Gaillard.

CHAPTER SEVEN

1. Parsch, op. cit., Band II, pp. 362-363.
2. Cf. Nocent, op. cit., Vol. 3, p. 164.
3. Adam, op. cit., p. 84.
4. Pope St. Leo, *Sermo* 76, 3.
5. Pope St. Leo, ibid.

CHAPTER EIGHT

1. St. Basil in *In Pos.*, 28, 7.
2. St. Gregory of Nyssa, *De precatione*, or. 2 MG 50, 779 f.
3. W.A. Jurgens, *General Instruction on the Liturgy of the Hours* (The Liturgical Press, Collegeville, Minn.), p. 35.
4. G.M. Hopkins, "Outline of a Sermon."
5. A.M. Roguet, O.P., *The Liturgy of the Hours* (The Liturgical Press, Collegeville, Minn.), p. 82.
6. Ibid., p. 82.